The Mason Jar
SOUP•to•NUTS
COOKBOOK

LONNETTE PARKS

SQUAREONE
PUBLISHERS

COVER DESIGNER: Phaedra Mastrocola
COVER PHOTO: Phaedra Mastrocola
IN-HOUSE EDITOR: Marie Caratozzolo
TYPESETTER: Gary A. Rosenberg

Square One Publishers
115 Herricks Road
Garden City Park, NY 11040
(516) 535-2010 • (877) 900-BOOK
www.squareonepublishers.com

Library of Congress Cataloging-in-Publication Data

Parks, Lonnette.
    The mason jar soup to nuts cookbook : how to create mason jar
recipe mixes / Lonnette Parks.
        p. cm.
    Includes index.
    ISBN 0-7570-0129-7 (pbk.)
    1. Cookery. 2. Food presentation. I. Title.
TX714 .P145   2004
641.5—dc22

                                                        2003020474

Contents

Cookies and Cakes

Soups and Stews

Beverages

I dedicate this book to Mike, my OAO.
Your unconditional love and huge support
have been outstanding.
Thank you for everything you are to me.
You are my world.
Forever and ever. Amen.

Acknowledgments

I must extend a special thank you to the folks at Square One Publishers—Rudy, Joanne, Marie, Bob, and Anthony—for making the creation of this book possible. I am also very grateful to kitchen testers Leslie and Ellen for their invaluable input. For her many ideas and recipe contributions, I'd also like to thank my best friend, Di, who, along with her family, was also my helpful taste-tester. Finally, I must acknowledge my three beautiful children—Kurtis, Nathan, and Bethany—who are a constant source of inspiration. I love you so much.

Introduction

The popularity of Mason jar mixes is taking the country by storm! These beautifully decorated jars are filled with attractive layers of ingredients for making a variety of kitchen creations. Topped with an eye-catching square of fabric that is tied on with decorative twine or ribbon, these jars are a pleasure to give and a joy to receive.

If you have ever wanted to create beautiful Mason gift jars in your own home, or try your hand at making the recipes yourself, here's the good news: You don't have to be a craft expert to assemble the containers, nor do you have to be a culinary school graduate to make the recipes in your own kitchen. *The Mason Jar Soup-to-Nuts Cookbook* will show you just how easy it is. Within its pages, you'll find recipes for satisfying soups and stews, delicious hot and cold beverages, and a sensational array of blue-ribbon baked goods. (Just for fun, it even includes a recipe for making "doggie" treats for your favorite four-legged friend!)

The book begins with a chapter called "The Basics." The first part of this chapter guides you in buying the best ingredients and equipment for your cooking adventures, and provides tips for successful recipe results. It then covers all the ins and outs of creating the jars, including what size jar to use, how to make neat, even ingredient layers, and how to add those finishing touches that turn the jar into a beautiful gift.

Next, you'll find over fifty kitchen-tested recipes that fall into the following categories: Breakfast Fare; Muffins, Scones, and Breads; Cookies and Cakes; Soups and Stews; and Beverages. There are heavenly baked treats like Apricot-Walnut Muffins and Blueberry Scones, breakfast dishes like Old World Muesli and Apple-Cinnamon Pancakes, and a tasty assortment of cookies including Toffee Chip and buttery Scottish Shortbread. You can also kick back and relax with a steaming mug of Café Mocha, or cool down with a frosty glass of Southern Peach Tea. And if it's heartier fare you're after, you can choose from an array of nourishing soups and stews, from Hearty Potato-Bean to Gobble-Up Turkey Noodle.

Because this book is designed for both the cook *and* the crafter, each recipe contains both instructions for making the recipe itself, and directions for creating the jarred mix—either to display in your own home or to present as gifts. A helpful diagram shows you how to layer the ingredients for attractive results, and a box neatly displays the recipe preparation instructions to include on your gift tag. All you have to do is pour the contents of the jar into a bowl or pot, add a few basic ingredients like butter and eggs, and follow a handful of easy instructions.

Whether you want to prepare the Mason jar recipes for your personal eating pleasure, or you'd like to create impressive gift jars for family and friends, *The Mason Jar Soup-to-Nuts Cookbook* is all you need. Enjoy the experience!

The**Basics**

Nothing warms the heart like home cooking! From pancakes and muffins to soups and smoothies, this book will show you just how easy it is to turn a few basic ingredients into a wealth of scrumptious culinary creations. You can whip up a stack of fluffy Apple-Cinnamon Pancakes to kick off the day, bake some Golden Pecan Muffins to enjoy with a cup of creamy Bavarian Mint Coffee during a midday break, and greet the kids with fresh batch of Toffee Chip Cookies as they walk through the door after a "tough day" at school. And with minimal effort, you can even prepare a pot of savory soup or stew, like Beefy Bean or Barley Rice, for a dinner that will have your family clamoring for seconds. Just as important, *The Mason Jar Soup-to-Nuts Cookbook* will guide you in making beautiful Mason jar mixes that will put the gift of home baking and cooking at the fingertips of friends and family.

While Mason jar mixes—and the recipes themselves—are a snap to make, you'll enjoy the best results if you keep a few guidelines in mind as you select ingredients, create your jar mixes, and then turn those

mixes into wonderful homemade treats. This chapter provides all the basics, insuring that both your Mason jar mixes and their tasty results are the best they can be.

INGREDIENTS

All of the ingredients used in *The Mason Jar Soup-to-Nuts Cookbook* are common, easy-to-find items. Many of these ingredients, such as flour and sugar, are used in the majority of baked goods found in this book. Others, such as dried beans and peas, are called for in many of the soups and stews. Because these products are important to recipe success, let's take a few minutes to learn more about them, so that you can choose the best ingredients possible.

Flour

If stored carelessly, flour can absorb moisture, affecting the outcome of your Mason jar cookies, cakes, and other baked goods. To keep your flour at its freshest, store it in a clean airtight container, and place the container in a cool place.

Most of the recipes for baked goods in this book call for all-purpose flour, which is a blend of refined hard and soft wheat flours. Choose either bleached or unbleached varieties, as either one will produce delicious results. The difference is only that the latter type has not undergone a bleaching process, and so contains more vitamin E than its bleached counterpart.

Once opened, flour will stay fresh for up to six months. Simply keep it in a clean, airtight container that prevents the product from absorbing any moisture, and store it in a cool place.

Granulated Sugar

Whenever the word "sugar" is used in this book, the recipe calls for granulated white sugar—although you may also use a super-granulated (superfine) sugar, which is a finer grind that is still coarse enough to have easily discernible crystals. White sugar is generally used when you want to enhance sweetness without adding the molasses-like flavor of brown sugar. When baking cookies, it is the sweetener of choice when a crisp cookie is desired.

Store your sugar as you would store flour—in a clean, airtight container kept in a cool place.

Brown Sugar

Brown sugar is simply granulated white sugar that has been coated with a film of molasses, and so is more flavorful than its white counterpart. Unless a specific type is called for in the recipe, you can use either light or dark brown sugar when making your Mason jar treats—the choice is yours. Just be aware that in addition to being darker in color, dark brown sugar has a more pronounced flavor than light.

Because brown sugar is moister than white sugar, when it is used to make cookies, the results will tend to be delightfully chewy. Be aware, though, that the same moisture that makes brown sugar so irresistible also makes it prone to turn hard and lumpy. To keep your purchase from turning into a rock-hard mass, be sure to store it in an airtight container (doubled zip-lock plastic bags are great) and to keep it in a cool place. If the sugar should become hard, however, simply microwave it, uncovered, for twenty to thirty seconds, or until it becomes soft enough to use with ease.

If your brown sugar turns hard, don't panic—and don't toss it out. Just heat the sugar in a microwave oven for twenty to thirty seconds, and it will become soft enough to use with ease.

Eggs

Eggs help provide the structural framework for many baked goods, helping them to rise. For best results when making the recipes in this book, use eggs marked "large" and buy the freshest ones you can find. Then refrigerate them and use them before the expiration date.

Butter

For the best flavor and texture, I use only pure sweet (unsalted) butter in my recipes for baked goods. If you prefer, you may substitute margarine for the butter, but don't use light butter, light margarine, or diet spreads, as all of these products contain added moisture that will adversely affect the finished products.

You'll find that the recipes in this book usually express butter amounts in terms of cups (½ cup, ¼ cup, etc.) These amounts are easy to measure, as one stick of butter (¼ pound) equals ½ cup, or eight tablespoons. For many recipes in this book, the ingredients list specifies softened butter. To soften the butter, simply allow it to sit at room temperature for forty-five minutes. However, don't leave it out of the refrigerator too long especially when making cookies. Overly soft butter will result in excessive spreading during the baking process. In fact, butter that is too warm *or* too cold can actually alter the temperature of the dough, affecting baking times.

Butter can be stored in either the refrigerator or the freezer. Kept in the refrigerator, butter remains fresh for up to two weeks; in the freezer, for up to six months.

Baking Soda and Baking Powder

The majority of Mason jar recipes that require leavening agents contain one or both of two common forms—baking soda and baking powder.

Also called bicarbonate of soda and sodium bicarbonate, baking soda is a naturally occurring substance. When used alone, baking soda has no leavening power. However, when used in a batter that also contains an acidic ingredient, such as molasses or buttermilk, it causes baked goods to rise.

Baking powder is a mixture of baking soda and other ingredients, the most important of which is an acidic compound such as cream of tartar. When this product is mixed in a batter with wet ingredients, leavening occurs. No acidic ingredients are needed, as the acid is already in the powder.

Why do the recipes in this book sometimes use one of these products and sometimes use both? Clearly, when no acidic ingredient is used in the batter, baking powder is the leavening of choice. But other factors may also come into play. For instance, when baking cookies in which lighter-colored puffier varieties are desired, baking powder is most appropriate. And baking soda can be used to lend a somewhat salty flavor to baked products.

Both baking soda and baking powder are inexpensive and readily available. Stored in covered containers, they will remain fresh and potent for up to six months.

Vanilla Extract

Many of the baked items in this book are flavored with vanilla extract. In preparing your Mason jar recipes, try to use only extract that is labeled "pure." Imitation extracts are composed of artificial ingredients, and often have a bitter aftertaste. These products can be used, of course, but since a bottle of extract lasts a long time, it makes sense to spend a little more and buy the best.

When extracts are called for in recipes, always choose varieties that are labeled "pure." Imitation extracts may save you a few cents, but they are composed of artificial ingredients that often leave a bitter aftertaste.

Oatmeal

In a variety of cookie and muffin recipes in *The Mason Jar Soup-to-Nuts Cookbook*, oatmeal is added for its distinctive yet subtle flavor and wonderfully chewy texture. For the most part, I use quick-cooking oats, as I find that they produce the best results. This product will stay fresh for up to six months when stored in a clean airtight container.

Nuts

Due to their oil content, nuts are a highly perishable ingredient. Unless you bake often, buy nuts in small amounts and store any leftovers in the refrigerator or freezer.

Many recipes in this book call for a variety of nuts—including walnuts, pecans, and almonds—to add flavor and crunch to baked goods. Feel free to replace one type of nut with another, according to your preferences. However, whenever the recipe specifies almonds, it is suggested that you avoid substituting other nuts simply because almonds have such a special and distinctive flavor—one that cannot be replaced by any other nut.

When toasted nuts are called for in a recipe, I simply place the nuts (shells removed) in a single layer on an ungreased baking sheet, and pop them into a 275 °F oven for about fifteen minutes, or until they are crisp and golden brown. It's important to keep an eye on the nuts as they toast, stirring them occasionally to prevent burning. Remove the toasted nuts from the oven and allow them to cool before chopping or crushing according to recipe instructions. Nuts must be cooled completely before they are used in a recipe or added to a Mason gift jar.

The flavor of nuts is carried by their essential oils, which is the same component that makes all nuts perishable. If you buy nuts in shells, they'll stay fresher, as the shells will protect them from air, moisture, heat, and light. In fact, unshelled nuts can be stored for about twice as long as shelled nuts. If the nuts are already shelled, though, place them in an airtight container and keep the container in a cool, dry, dark place for up to two months before using. To increase the nuts' shelf life, place the container in the refrigerator, where they'll stay fresh for up to four months, or in the freezer, where they can remain for up to six months.

Chocolate Chips

Chocolate chips are used to add color, creaminess, and flavor to a number of Mason jar recipes ranging from pancakes and muffins to cookies and breads. You will, of course, get the best results when you opt for the highest-quality product available. I always use the purest chocolate chips—never chips that are labeled "imitation" chocolate. Although a bit more pricey, pure chocolate chips result in a truer chocolate flavor as well as a creamier texture.

If you use only a portion of a bag of chocolate chips, wrap the remaining chips tightly and store in a cool (60°F to 70°F), dry place. If kept in a warm environment, the chocolate may develop pale gray steaks and blotches as the cocoa butter rises to the surface. In damp conditions, chocolate may form tiny gray sugar crystals on the surface. In either case, the chocolate can still be used, but flavor and texture will be slightly affected. Note that because of the milk solids found in both milk and white chocolate, these chips should be stored for no longer than nine months. Dark chocolate, though, can remain fresh for up to *ten years* when properly stored.

Beans and Peas

A number of Mason jar soups include dried legumes—peas and beans.

Chocolate chips add flavor, color, and creamy goodness to a variety of baked goods. Avoid using imitation varieties, which, like imitation extracts, do not deliver the best flavor. To insure that your cookies, muffins, and other sweet treats taste as good as they look, use only pure chocolate chips.

In addition to their flavor and texture, these tasty morsels are nutritional powerhouses. They are fat- and cholesterol-free, and provide healthy amounts of B vitamins, protein, complex carbohydrates, iron, and potassium. Because they are a natural product, packages of dried legumes may contain some that are shriveled or discolored. Before cooking peas or beans, or layering them in the Mason jar, be sure to discard those that are blemished or discolored.

A number of the dried beans called for in the Mason jar soup and stew recipes benefit greatly from presoaking. This step allows beans to slowly absorb the moisture needed to cook evenly, while greatly reducing their cooking time. Furthermore, presoaking aids digestion by breaking down the beans' oligosaccharides—the indigestible sugars that cause gas and bloating.

Some of the legumes called for in this book, such as lentils and split peas, cook quickly—within thirty to forty-five minutes. Others, including kidney, navy, and black beans, should be presoaked, which greatly reduces cooking time, and allows the beans to slowly absorb the moisture needed to cook evenly. Presoaking also keeps beans from splitting open or from the having the outside shell fall apart while the middle remains hard. Soaking also helps break down the beans' oligosaccharides (the indigestible sugars that cause gas), aiding in digestion. Although beans may vary in size and shape, they benefit from two basic soaking methods—long-soaking and quick-soaking.

For the long-soaking method, place the beans in a large bowl or pot, and cover them with four times as much boiling water. Soak the beans for eight to twelve hours, or as specified in the recipe. Once soaked, discard the water and rinse with fresh.

When time is a factor, you can use one or two quick-soaking methods. Place the beans in a pot along with four times as much water. Bring the pot to a boil over high heat, and continue to boil for two minutes. Remove the pot from the heat, cover, and let stand for one hour. You can also presoak beans using your microwave. Simply place the beans in a microwave-safe container, cover with four times the amount of water, and microwave on high power for fifteen minutes, or until the water boils. Remove from the oven, cover, and let soak for one hour.

You may find that some beans refuse to soften. You can soak them for hours and hours, and then simmer them all day long, but they're still rock hard. This is typically characteristic of beans that are very old or ones that have been improperly stored. Beans that are exposed to high temperatures and humidity undergo chemical changes that make them almost impossible to soften. To avoid this, keep dried beans in an airtight container and store in a cool dry place.

BASIC KITCHEN EQUIPMENT

Only the simplest of kitchen equipment is needed to create delicious Mason jar recipes, whether you're baking cookies or making soup. Using the right tools for the job will help you enjoy success each and every time you select a recipe from this book.

Measuring Cups and Spoons

The accurate measuring of ingredients is essential to baking and cooking success. And the key to accurate measuring is the use of basic measuring cups and spoons.

When measuring dry ingredients such as flour, sugar, and oatmeal, always use dry measuring cups. Available in sets that usually include 1-cup, ½-cup, ⅓-cup, and ¼-cup measures, these cups allow you to spoon or scoop up the ingredient and then level it off with a straight edge—a metal spatula or knife—for greatest accuracy. *Never* use a liquid measuring cup for this purpose as it will make precise measuring impossible. When measuring liquid ingredients such as milk, applesauce, or melted butter, be sure to use liquid measuring cups, which are

Be sure to use nested metal or plastic cups to measure dry ingredients, and graduated glass or plastic cups to measure liquids. Never use liquid measuring cups for flour, as you could end up adding an extra tablespoon or more per cup!

clear cups with markings that indicate ¼-, ⅓-, ½-, ⅔-, and ¾-cup levels. For greatest accuracy, place the cup on the counter and bend down to check the amount at eye level.

Always use measuring spoons—not the teaspoons and tablespoons you use to set your table—to measure small amounts of spices, dried herbs, and the like. These inexpensive tools come in sets that usually include 1-tablepoon, 1-teaspoon, ½-teaspoon, and ¼-teaspoon measures. When using dry ingredients, if possible, dip the spoon in the container until it overflows, and then gently shake the spoon to level it off. When measuring wet ingredients, pour the liquid until it reaches the top edge of the spoon.

Mixing Bowls

Mixing bowls can be made of a variety of materials, including stainless steel, glass, ceramic, and plastic. While all of these are good choices, tempered glass bowls have an added advantage—they allow you to easily see when the ingredients are well mixed; furthermore, you can microwave ingredients, such as chocolate, in them.

Especially when preparing the doughs and batters for your Mason jar cakes, cookies, and other baked treats, you'll need just a few different mixing bowls. A small bowl of about 1 quart in size will be called for just occasionally to hold a sugary topping or another single ingredient. More commonly, you'll want a medium-sized bowl (about 2 quarts) and a large bowl (about 3 quarts).

Mixing bowls can be made of a variety of materials, including glass, stainless steel, plastic, and ceramic. If you don't already own a set of bowls, consider buying tempered glass. Glass bowls not only allow you to easily see when the ingredients are well mixed, but also make it possible to microwave ingredients such as chocolate.

Electric Mixers

While an electric mixer is not a baking necessity, if you do have one on hand, it will make quick work of creaming butter, and, in some recipes, mixing batter or dough. Either a portable (hand-held) or a stationary (stand) mixer can be used—although I personally like a portable model. If you don't have a mixer, just use a sturdy wooden spoon or whisk— and a little elbow grease, of course.

Baking (Cookie) Sheets

Every baker has personal preferences regarding baking sheets. For cookie baking, I feel that I get the best results with air cushion sheets, which are made of two layers of metal with a "layer" of air in between. The dual layered sheets allow air to better circulate under the cookie-baking surface, reducing hot spots so that cookies bake beautifully all across the sheet, and not just in the middle. These sheets come with both nonstick and regular surfaces. Either surface will yield great results.

Composed of two sheets of metal with a layer of air in between, air cushion baking sheets reduce hot spots so that cookies bake beautifully all across the sheet.

To insure even baking, use a cookie sheet that fits in the oven with at least one inch to spare around each edge. Whether or not your sheet is nonstick, it is not necessary to grease the baking surface unless it is called for in the recipe. When greasing is recommended, either coat the pan lightly with cooking spray, or rub a small amount of butter or shortening evenly over the bottom.

Baking (Cake) Pans

Baking pans come in all sorts of shapes and sizes. Over the years, I have accumulated quite a variety; however, I find that I get the most mileage out of just a few. The cake and bar cookie recipes in this book require an 8-inch square, a 9-inch round, or a 9-x-13-inch rectangular-shaped pan. Bundt cakes need a 12-cup (10-inch) bundt pan, and the breads are baked in 9-x-5-inch loaf pans. For the muffins, a standard tin for making 3-inch muffins is required.

Baking pans come with both nonstick and regular surfaces. Whether or not your pans are nonstick, it is not necessary to grease the baking surface unless it is called for in the recipe. As with the cookie sheets, when greasing is recommended, either coat the pan lightly with cooking spray, or rub a small amount of butter or shortening evenly over its bottom and sides.

Baking Racks

Most of the instructions for baked goods in this book direct you to first allow the freshly baked cookies or cakes to cool on the baking sheet or in the pan for about five minutes. (If removed too soon, hot cookies fresh from the oven may lose their shape, while cakes and muffins have a tendency to crack or break apart.) Once they have cooled a bit, these baked treats should be removed and placed on a baking rack for further cooling. Made of wire, these racks speed the cooling process by allowing air to flow around both the tops and bottoms of freshly baked items. In most cases, your Mason jar creations will be ready for serving or storage within twenty minutes.

If you don't own cooling racks, you can, of course, simply transfer the cookies or cakes directly to a plate. Be aware, though, that the moisture from the heat may cause these baked goods to slightly adhere to the plate.

Soup Pots

When preparing soups and stews, choosing the right cooking vessel

Whenever a cookie recipe directs you to grease the baking sheet, a great alternative is to line it with baker's parchment paper. Available in supermarkets and specialty stores, this paper not only prevents sticking, but also saves on clean-up time.

is important. One key to determining quality stovetop cookware is weight. Heavy-gauge pots and pans distribute heat more evenly than thinner ones, which tend to scorch food more easily. When it comes to preparing soups and slow-cooking stews, stainless steel or cast-iron pots with heavy bottoms are the best. The recipes in this book call for either a medium-sized (4-quart) or large (6-quart) pot or Dutch oven, depending on the yield.

Because they promote even heat distribution and minimize scorching, stainless steel or cast iron pots with heavy bottoms are the optimal choice for cooking soups and slow-simmering stews.

BAKING AND COOKING TIPS

The Mason jar recipes are easy to follow for even the beginning baker or novice cook. Just keep a few simple guidelines in mind, and you're sure to find success with every recipe you select.

Measuring the Ingredients

Earlier in the chapter, I mentioned the importance of accurately measuring ingredients to achieve successful cooking and baking results (see page 11). In addition to following the basic guidelines presented in that discussion, keep these tips in mind when preparing the recipes in this book.

❏ There's no need to sift the flour before—or after—measuring it for any of the recipes. But keep in mind that the amount of flour used in baked goods is crucial, so care should be taken to avoid adding more flour than recommended. To keep the flour light and the measurement true, either dip the cup in the flour bin or spoon the flour into the cup before leveling with a straight edge, such as a spatula or knife.

When measuring butter, remember that a 1/4-pound stick equals 1/2 cup, or 8 tablespoons. Usually, the butter wrapper has tablespoons clearly marked, making it easy to measure out the proper amount.

❑ When measuring butter, soften the butter only until it is malleable enough to be packed into a dry measuring cup. Then level off the top with a straight edge.

❑ Measure brown sugar by packing it firmly into a dry measuring cup and leveling it off with a straight edge. When the sugar is turned out of the cup, it should hold its shape.

❑ When measuring raisins and other soft, chunky ingredients, press them into the measuring cup. When measuring dry, chunky ingredients—chocolate chips and chopped nuts, for instance—spoon the ingredient into the cup, tap the cup against the table to make the ingredients settle, and add more if necessary.

Mixing the Batter or Dough

Most of the Mason jar cookie and cake recipes require that you cream or blend the butter with one or more of the other ingredients, such as the vanilla extract or the egg. This is an important step because it helps insure the proper ingredient blending of the dough or batter. It also incorporates air into the mixture, enabling your baking soda and baking powder do their work. Although I use a portable mixer to cream the required ingredients, this step can also be performed with a whisk, fork, or a wooden spoon. Just keep mixing or beating until the ingredients are blended according to recipe instructions.

Once the butter mixture has been blended, most recipes will direct you to add the dry ingredients to this mixture. In some cases, the ingredients can be combined with either a wooden spoon or an electric mixer set on low speed. Be aware, though, that when the dry ingredients include chocolate chips or other goodies that might be chopped up by an electric mixer, it's best to use a spoon.

Forming and Baking Cookies

Some of the Mason jar cookies in this book are drop cookies, meaning that you form the cookies by scooping the dough up with a teaspoon and dropping it onto the baking sheet. Cookie doughs vary in consistency. Some will fall easily from the spoon, while others may need a push from your finger or a second spoon. To make the cookies uniform in size, use a measuring teaspoon rather than the teaspoon from your everyday flatware, and scoop up a heaping teaspoonful.

Cookie dough that needs to be rolled out and cut must be relatively stiff. If the dough seems too soft and sticky, refrigerate it for twenty minutes or so. Then *lightly* dust the work surface with a little flour, and use a rolling pin to form the dough into a sheet of the correct thickness. If sticking continues to be a problem, you can also dust the rolling pin with a little flour. Don't use too much flour, though, as an excessive amount will result in a tough cookie. After cutting the dough, press the remaining pieces together into a ball. Return the dough to the refrigerator until it is firm enough to roll and cut.

As the cookies are formed—whether "drop" type or "cut"—place them at least two inches apart on your cookie sheet to allow for spreading. It is not necessary to grease the baking sheet unless the recipe specifically directs you to do so. Bake only one cookie sheet at a time, and make sure the sheet is on the middle rack of the oven with at least one inch between the edge of the pan and the oven itself. This will promote proper airflow and even heating.

Although electric mixers can sometimes be used to blend wet and dry ingredients, whenever a dough or batter contains chocolate chips or other chunky ingredients that you want to remain whole, you'll enjoy best results by mixing with a wooden spoon.

Checking for Doneness of Baked Goods

Baking times vary from oven to oven, and can even differ because of variations in ingredients. For best results, check your cakes and cookies for doneness at the minimum baking time.

Most cakes, muffins, and breads are finished baking when a toothpick inserted into their center comes out dry. As mentioned earlier, once they are removed from the oven, these piping hot cakes should be allowed to sit for five to ten minutes before they are released from their pans. If removed too soon, the cake may crack or crumble apart.

Baking time for cookies is much shorter than it is for most other baked goods. In most cases, cookies are done when they are slightly browned around the edges. Since baking time and oven temperature affect the cookie's final texture, you may also choose to make adjustments according to your personal preferences. If you want your cookies to be chewy, slightly underbake them. If you want them to be crisp, bake them a little longer. A watchful eye is very important when baking cookies, as they can quickly turn from *done* to *burned*.

Keep in mind that most ovens run either a little hotter or a little cooler than the temperature to which they're set, so be aware that you may have to compensate by adjusting either the temperature to which the oven is set or the baking time. (If desired, use an oven thermometer to determine the precise temperature.)

Doubling or Halving the Recipes

Some of the recipes in this book provide instructions for creating quart-sized Mason gift jars, while others are designed for pint-sized containers. The soup and beverage recipes can be easily doubled or halved. However, when it comes to baked goods, successful recipe conversion is often more complicated than simply multiplying or dividing ingredient amounts. Doing so may alter delicate chemical reactions—with possible disastrous results. Because all of the Mason jar recipes have been successfully kitchen tested as they are presented in this book, I recommend preparing them and creating gift jars exactly as instructed.

CREATING THE JARS

Although you'll enjoy making the recipes found in this book, you'll also take pleasure in giving Mason jar mixes to friends and family. These mixes make perfect gifts.

Fortunately, Mason jar mixes are easy—and fun—to create. Below, you'll learn about the few simple materials you'll need to get started, and you'll discover how to use them to craft beautiful mixes that are a joy to give and receive.

Choosing the Materials

The materials needed to make Mason jar mixes are inexpensive and few in number. Keep these items on hand, and you'll be able to create a gift at a moment's notice.

The Jar

For each mix you make, you will need a clean, dry, Mason jar—in either a quart or pint size, depending on the recipe. While other screw-top containers may also be suitable, the large opening of a Mason jar will give you the room you need to pour in the ingredients, tamp them down into even layers, and periodically wipe the inside of the jar with a dry paper towel during filling so that the final gift has a neat, clean appearance.

The recipe mixes presented in this book can be packed in a variety of jars, but the wide mouth of a Mason-type jar makes it easy to create neat, attractive layers of ingredients.

The Fabric and Tie

When you finish filling your Mason jar with dry ingredients that are either premixed or placed in attractive layers, the container will be instantly transformed into an attractive gift. Many people, in fact, use the unadorned jars to decorate their kitchens and pantries! But you can further enhance the charm of the mix by tying a square of decorative fabric to the top.

When looking for fabrics to trim the top of your Mason jar mix, be sure to check the remnants pile at your local fabric or crafts store. Often, you'll be able to decorate a number of gifts for just a few dollars.

For each quart-sized jar, you will need a seven-by-seven-inch piece of fabric, cut with either regular fabric scissors or pinking shears. Pint-sized jars require a six-by-six-inch square. When choosing your fabric, be creative. A square of denim, burlap, or calico would create a delightful country look, for instance, while a red-and-green fabric would be the perfect finishing touch for a Christmas gift. Often, fabric stores offer inexpensive remnants, each of which could adorn several jars.

Be sure to select a tie that complements your fabric. A length of sisal twine or yarn would make an appropriate tie for your calico square, for example, while a slender gold or silver ribbon would beautifully complete your holiday gift. Just make sure the tie is long enough. A forty-eight-inch length will allow you to securely attach the fabric, as well as your tag, to the jar.

The Tag

Your tag will provide the all-important information that the recipient of the jar will need to turn the jar mix into a delicious homemade treat. Each tag should supply the name of the recipe, the yield of the recipe, the list of ingredients that must be added to the mix (eggs and butter, for instance), and the preparation instructions themselves.

Feel free to make a no-fuss tag or to craft one that showcases your creativity and flair. Each recipe contains a boxed copy of the information that belongs on its tag. If you like, you can simply make a photocopy of this box, using the paper of your choice; cut the photocopy out with plain scissors or pinking shears; and attach the printed tag to your jar with the selected tie. Or you may choose to cut out a piece of sturdy paper—a three-by-four-inch size is usually adequate—and write out the instructions in your own clear handwriting or in calligraphy. If you have a computer, of course, your options are even greater. Consider typing in the instructions and printing them out in a beautiful (but readable) font. Add a decorative border, if you wish. You can even print the instructions directly onto stickers and affix a sticker to each jar in place of a tag. The possibilities are endless.

Adding the Ingredients

With the exception of the beverage recipes and the recipes for waffles, pancakes, and oatmeal—which require the dry ingredients to be pre-mixed—all of the recipes in this book include ingredients that can be attractively layered in the Mason jars. Believe it or not, the order in which the ingredients are packed in these jars can make a *big* difference. Imagine, for instance, pouring the granulated sugar over a layer of chocolate chips. Gradually, the sugar will sift between the chips, mixing the layers and creating a messy appearance. That's why the white sugar is so often placed over a layer of brown sugar or oatmeal.

By following the order prescribed in the "Creating the Jar" section of each recipe, you will be sure to put together an attractive jar. Be aware, though, that in most cases, this is not the *only* way in which the

The tag for your gift jar can be as simple or as creative as you like. For a fuss-free tag, just photocopy the boxed instructions provided in the recipe. Other options include writing the directions out in calligraphy and generating tags or labels on your home computer. Just make sure that your gift tag includes the name of the recipe, the yield of the recipe, the list of ingredients that must be added to the mix, and the preparation instructions.

ingredients can be successfully layered. I have usually chosen to provide you with the simplest method of packing the jar. If you prefer to arrange the layers differently, go for it! After you make a few gift jars, you'll get a feel for the process. To keep your layers as neat as possible, just remember to avoid placing powdery or granular ingredients— flour and sugar, for instance—above a product such as chocolate chips, nuts, or raisins. Because chips and the like have space between the individual pieces, they will allow the powdery substance to sift in. Instead, try to pack an ingredient such as brown sugar above these goodies, as the moist sugar will form a "seal," preventing the layers from blending together.

Some of the soup and stew recipes contain jar ingredients, such as pasta or egg noodles, that are to be added to the pot *after* the other ingredients have been cooking for a while. (Imagine how pasta would become if it were allowed to cook in a soup for more than thirty minutes? Does the image of "mush" come to mind?) For recipes in which this occurs, you will be instructed to place the pasta or other "to-be-added-later" ingredient in a resealable sandwich bag before placing it in the jar. This will keep it separate from the other items.

When placing ingredients into the Mason jar, especially flour, cocoa, and other powdery ingredients, you might find a wide-mouth canning funnel to be a helpful tool. Placed over the top of the jar, this functional piece of equipment helps guide the ingredients into the jar easily and neatly. Made of plastic or stainless steel, canning funnels are found at most stores that sell kitchen tools and gadgets. You can also purchase funnels online at sites such as www.cooking.com and www.DoItBest. com. It is also easy to make your own canning funnel. Just follow the simple steps presented on the next page.

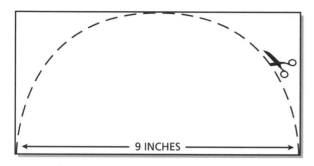

1. Cut a 9-inch semi-circle out of oak tag or other stiff paper.

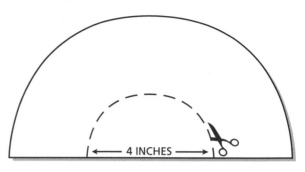

2. Cut a 4-inch semi-circle from the center of the paper, as shown above.

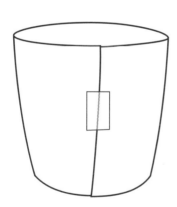

3. Bring the two sides together and attach with tape.

Making a Wide-Mouth Funnel

4. Voila!

After adding each ingredient to your Mason jar, press the addition into a firm, level layer with a flat-bottomed object, such as a tart tamper or the bottom of a long, narrow drinking glass. After tamping down powdery ingredients, like flour or cocoa, use a paper towel to wipe the inside of the jar—removing any powder that may be clinging to the glass—before pouring in the next ingredient.

As you create your Mason jar mixes, be sure to pack the ingredients firmly. After pouring in each ingredient, use a long-handled tart tamper; the squeezable bulb section of a turkey baster; or the bottom of a long, slim drinking glass to press the addition into an even layer. Then, before adding the next ingredient, wipe the inside of the jar with a dry paper towel to achieve a clean, professional appearance.

After all the layers of the jar mix have been added, simply screw on the top of the jar, tightening it as much as possible to keep the mixture fresh. Now you're ready to complete the gift.

Decorating the Jar

To add the finishing touches to your jarred mix, simply center the chosen fabric square on the lid of the jar and secure it with a rubber band. Then wrap your chosen tie around the rubber band twice, covering the band, and knot the tie to hold it in place.

Using a hole punch, make a hole in the tag and slide the tie through the hole, threading it through once or twice and tying it off with a bow. If you've chosen to photocopy the boxed tag provided with each recipe, you may want to fold the left side of the tag over the right before punching a hole in the top left-hand corner. This will allow you to thread the tie through two layers of paper, attaching your tag securely to the jar.

Finally, to make your Mason gift jar even more special, you may want to use the same ribbon or twine to attach an item that can be used when preparing the particular recipe. Wooden spoons, wire whisks, and cookie cutters are possible choices. Your beautiful Mason jar mix is now done, ready for its lucky recipient!

Best Ever Chocolate Chip Cookies

HOW TO USE THIS BOOK

The Mason Jar Soup-to-Nuts Cookbook has a unique format that allows you to easily prepare the recipes in your kitchen or create beautiful Mason jar mixes.

First, use the table of contents or the index to choose a recipe that suits your fancy. With the exception of the beverages, which are found at the end of the book, you will find that the directions for each recipe fall on two facing pages. On the left-hand page, you'll find instructions for preparing the recipes at home. On the right-hand page, you'll find instructions for creating a Mason jar mix.

If you have decided to bake a tray of cookies, for instance, simply look at the left-hand page of the two-page recipe spread. You'll see that the ingredients have been broken into two lists. The first list—the Jar Ingredients—contains the nonperishable ingredients that would be placed in the jar if you were creating a mix. These items have been grouped together here for ease of mixing, as in most cases, all the Jar Ingredients get combined first. The second list presents the Additional Ingredients—the eggs, butter, and other perishable items that must be added to the dry mix. The numbered instructions will tell you exactly how to prepare the recipe.

If your goal is to craft a gift jar, look at the right-hand page. The numbered instructions at the top of the page outline the steps for creating the jar. (For more details, see pages 19 to 24 of this chapter.) Next to these instructions, you'll find a diagram that shows you how to fill the jar for attractive results. (Just remember that the layer shown at the *bottom* of the diagram should be placed in the jar *first*.) Finally, at the bottom of the page, you'll find all the information you need for your

By following the diagram included in each recipe, you'll be sure to create an attractive Mason jar mix. Just remember to place the ingredient shown at the bottom of the diagram in the jar first.

tag. As discussed on page 21, you can photocopy the tag directly from the book and attach the copy to your jar, or, if you prefer, you can write these instructions out on decorative paper.

With *The Mason Jar Soup-to-Nuts Cookbook*, you can easily create a wealth of sweet treats, satisfying soups and stews, and delightful beverages that are sure to bring smiles to the faces of friends and family alike. What's more, you can also give the gift of beautiful Mason jar mixes to everyone on your gift list. Have fun!

BreakfastFare

APPLE-CINNAMON **PANCAKES**

When it comes to breakfast, pancakes are my favorite.
I find these apple-cinnamon pancakes especially irresistible,
especially when topped with butter and pure maple syrup.

YIELD:
4 SERVINGS
(4 PANCAKES EACH)

**QUART-SIZE JAR
INGREDIENTS**

3 cups all-purpose
flour

1/2 cup chopped
dried apples

3 tablespoons sugar

2 tablespoons
baking powder

4 1/2 teaspoons
ground cinnamon

1 1/4 teaspoons salt

**ADDITIONAL
INGREDIENTS
PER SERVING**

1 egg, slightly beaten

1/2 cup cold milk

1 tablespoon
vegetable oil

1. Combine all of the jar ingredients in a large bowl and set aside.

2. Lightly coat a nonstick griddle or large skillet with cooking spray, and place over medium-high heat.

3. Place 1 cup of the jar mixture in a medium-sized bowl. Add the egg, milk, and oil, and mix gently with a wooden spoon or whisk until well blended but slightly lumpy.

4. For each pancake, pour 1/3 cup of batter onto the hot griddle. Cook for 1 1/2 minutes, or until the top begins to bubble and the edges are dry and slightly brown. Flip the pancake over and cook another 30 to 45 seconds, or until the bottom is golden brown.

5. Serve hot with butter and syrup.

6. Transfer the remaining dry pancake mixture to the jar or another airtight container. Store in a cool dry place.

CREATING THE JAR

PREMIXING REQUIRED

3 cups all-purpose flour

$\frac{1}{2}$ cup chopped dried apples

3 tablespoons sugar

2 tablespoons baking powder

4 $\frac{1}{2}$ teaspoons ground cinnamon

1 $\frac{1}{4}$ teaspoons salt

1. Wash and thoroughly dry a 1-quart wide-mouth canning jar.

2. In a large bowl, combine all of the ingredients listed in the jar shown at left. *Premixing is required for this recipe.* Transfer the mixture to the canning jar.

3. Secure the lid, and decorate as desired (see page 24). Attach the instructions for making the pancakes found below.

Jar Yield:
4 servings
(4 pancakes each)

For each serving, in addition to 1 cup of jar mix, you will need to add:

1 egg, slightly beaten

$\frac{1}{2}$ cup cold milk

1 tablespoon vegetable oil

APPLE-CINNAMON PANCAKES

Lightly coat a nonstick griddle or large skillet with cooking spray, and place over medium-high heat. Place 1 cup of the jar mix in a medium-sized bowl. Add the egg, milk, and oil, and mix gently with a wooden spoon or whisk until well blended but slightly lumpy. Pour $\frac{1}{3}$ cups of batter onto the hot griddle and cook 1 $\frac{1}{2}$ minutes, or until bubbles form on top and the edges are dry and browned. Flip and cook another 30 seconds, or until the bottoms are golden brown. Serve hot with butter and syrup.

BUCKWHEATPANCAKES

The combination of whole wheat and buckwheat
gives these pancakes a nutritional boost.

YIELD:
4 SERVINGS
(4 PANCAKES EACH)

QUART-SIZE JAR
INGREDIENTS

2 cups buckwheat
flour

2 cups whole wheat
flour

1 teaspoon salt

2 tablespoons brown
sugar

4 teaspoons
baking powder

ADDITIONAL
INGREDIENTS
PER SERVING

1 egg, slightly beaten

1 cup cold milk

1 ½ teaspoons
vegetable oil

1. Combine all of the jar ingredients in a large bowl and set aside.

2. Lightly coat a nonstick griddle or large skillet with cooking spray, and place over medium-high heat.

3. Place 1 cup of the jar mixture in a medium-sized bowl. Add the egg, milk, and oil, and mix gently with a wooden spoon or whisk until well blended but slightly lumpy.

4. For each pancake, pour ½ cup of batter onto the hot griddle. Cook for 1½ minutes, or until the top begins to bubble and the edges are dry and slightly brown. Flip the pancake over and cook another 30 to 45 seconds, or until the bottom is golden brown.

5. Serve hot with butter and syrup.

6. Transfer the remaining dry pancake mixture to the jar or another airtight container. Store in a cool dry place.

CREATING THE JAR

1. Wash and thoroughly dry a 1-quart wide-mouth canning jar.

2. In a large bowl, combine all of the ingredients listed in the jar shown at left. *Premixing is required for this recipe.* Transfer the mixture to the canning jar.

3. Secure the lid, and decorate as desired (see page 24). Attach the instructions for making the pancakes found below.

PREMIXING REQUIRED

2 cups buckwheat flour

2 cups whole wheat flour

1 teaspoon salt

2 tablespoons brown sugar

4 teaspoons baking powder

Jar Yield:
4 servings
(4 pancakes each)

For each serving, in addition
to 1 cup of jar mix,
you will need to add:

1 egg, slightly beaten

1 cup cold milk

1 1/2 teaspoons vegetable oil

BUCKWHEAT PANCAKES

Lightly coat a nonstick griddle or large skillet with cooking spray, and place over medium-high heat. Place 1 cup of the jar mix in a medium-sized bowl. Add the egg, milk, and oil, and mix gently with a wooden spoon or whisk until well blended but slightly lumpy. Pour 1/2 cups of batter onto the hot griddle and cook 1 1/2 minutes, or until bubbles form on top and the edges are dry and browned. Flip and cook another 30 seconds, or until the bottoms are golden brown. Serve hot with butter and syrup.

CHOCOLATECHIPPANCAKES

My kids love these pancakes topped with
peanut butter and maple syrup.

YIELD:
4 SERVINGS
(4 PANCAKES EACH)

QUART-SIZE JAR INGREDIENTS

3 cups all-purpose flour

1 cup chocolate chips

3 tablespoons sugar

2 tablespoons baking powder

1 ¼ teaspoon salt

ADDITIONAL INGREDIENTS PER SERVING

1 egg, slightly beaten

½ cup cold milk

1 tablespoon vegetable oil

1. Combine all of the jar ingredients in a large bowl and set aside.

2. Lightly coat a nonstick griddle or large skillet with cooking spray, and place over medium-high heat.

3. Place 1 cup of the jar mixture in a medium-sized bowl. Add the egg, milk, and oil, and mix gently with a wooden spoon or whisk until well blended but slightly lumpy.

4. For each pancake, pour ⅓ cup of batter onto the hot griddle. Cook for 1½ minutes, or until the top begins to bubble and the edges are dry and slightly brown. Flip the pancake over and cook another 30 to 45 seconds, or until the bottom is golden brown.

5. Serve hot with butter and syrup.

6. Transfer the remaining dry pancake mixture to the jar or another airtight container. Store in a cool dry place.

CREATINGTHEJAR

1. Wash and thoroughly dry a 1-quart wide-mouth canning jar.

2. In a large bowl, combine all of the ingredients listed in the jar shown at left. *Premixing is required for this recipe.* Transfer the mixture to the canning jar.

3. Secure the lid, and decorate as desired (see page 24). Attach the instructions for making the pancakes found below.

PREMIXING REQUIRED

3 cups all-purpose flour

1 cup chocolate chips

3 tablespoons sugar

2 tablespoons baking powder

1 1/4 teaspoons salt

Jar Yield:
4 servings
(4 pancakes each)

For each serving, in addition to 1 cup of jar mix, you will need to add:

1 egg, slightly beaten

3/4 cup cold milk

2 tablespoons vegetable oil

CHOCOLATE CHIP PANCAKES

Lightly coat a nonstick griddle or large skillet with cooking spray, and place over medium-high heat. Place 1 cup of the jar mix in a medium-sized bowl. Add the egg, milk, and oil, and mix gently with a wooden spoon or whisk until well blended but slightly lumpy. Pour 1/3 cups of batter onto the hot griddle and cook 1 1/2 minutes, or until bubbles form on top and the edges are dry and browned. Flip and cook another 30 seconds, or until the bottoms are golden brown. Serve hot with butter and syrup.

AVERI'S APPLE OATMEAL

My friend's granddaughter Averi loves oatmeal.
So Averi's mom created this instant version,
which she conveniently packages in resealable plastic bags.
Now even Averi's dad can prepare her favorite breakfast in a snap.

YIELD:
8 SERVINGS
(½ CUP EACH)

**QUART-SIZE JAR
INGREDIENTS**

3 cups quick-cooking
oatmeal

½ cup coarsely
chopped dried apples

½ cup powdered
nondairy creamer

½ cup brown sugar

2 teaspoons
ground cinnamon

1 teaspoon salt

**ADDITIONAL
INGREDIENT
PER SERVING**

⅔ cup boiling water

1. Combine all of the jar ingredients in a large bowl.

2. Place ½ cup of the oatmeal mixture in a cereal bowl, add ⅔ cup boiling water, and stir gently until well mixed.

3. Let the oatmeal stand for 2 minutes to thicken, then stir again.

4. If desired, stir in some butter, cream, or additional brown sugar before serving.

5. Transfer the remaining dry oatmeal mixture to the jar or another airtight container. Store in a cool dry place.

CREATINGTHEJAR

3 cups quick-cooking oatmeal

1/2 cup coarsely chopped dried apples

1/2 cup powdered nondairy creamer

1/2 cup brown sugar

2 teaspoons ground cinnamon

1 teaspoon salt

1. Wash and thoroughly dry a 1-quart wide-mouth canning jar.

2. In a large bowl, combine all of the ingredients listed in the jar shown at left. *Premixing is required for this recipe.* Transfer the mixture to the canning jar.

3. Secure the lid, and decorate as desired (see page 24). Attach the instructions for making the oatmeal found below.

Jar Yield:
8 servings
(1/2 cup each)

For each serving, in addition to 1/2 cup of jar mix, you will need to add:

2/3 cup boiling water

AVERI'S APPLE OATMEAL

Place 1/2 cup of the jar mix in a cereal bowl. Add the boiling water and stir gently until well mixed. Let the oatmeal stand for 2 minutes to thicken, then stir again. If desired, stir in some butter, cream, or additional brown sugar before serving.

LIGHT'n FLUFFY
BUTTERMILK WAFFLES

These lighter-than-air waffles are worth getting out of bed for!

YIELD:
2 SERVINGS
(3 WAFFLES EACH)

QUART-SIZE JAR INGREDIENTS

2 cups all-purpose flour

1 1/4 cups buttermilk powder

1 cup nonfat dry milk

1/8 cup sugar

2 teaspoons baking powder

1 teaspoon baking soda

1/2 teaspoon salt

ADDITIONAL INGREDIENTS PER SERVING

1 egg, slightly beaten

3/4 cup + 2 tablespoons water

2 tablespoons vegetable oil

1. Combine all of the jar ingredients in a large bowl and set aside.

2. Preheat a lightly greased Belgian waffle iron.

3. Place 2 cups of the jar mixture in a medium-sized bowl. Add the egg, water, and oil, and mix gently with a wooden spoon or whisk until well blended.

4. For each waffle, pour 1/2 cup of batter onto the hot waffle iron, and cook until golden brown.

5. Serve hot with butter and syrup.

6. Transfer the remaining dry waffle mixture to the jar or another airtight container. Store in a cool dry place.

PREMIXING REQUIRED

2 cups all-purpose flour

1 ¼ cups buttermilk powder

1 cup nonfat dry milk

⅛ cup sugar

2 teaspoons baking powder

1 teaspoon baking soda

½ teaspoon salt

CREATING THE JAR

1. Wash and thoroughly dry a 1-quart wide-mouth canning jar.

2. In a large bowl, combine all of the ingredients listed in the jar at left. *Premixing is required for this recipe.* Transfer the mixture to the canning jar.

3. Secure the lid, and decorate as desired (see page 24). Attach the instructions for making the waffles found below.

Jar Yield:
2 servings
(3 waffles each)

For each serving, in addition to 2 cups of jar mix, you will need to add:

1 egg, slightly beaten

¾ cup + 2 tablespoons water

2 tablespoons vegetable oil

LIGHT 'N FLUFFY WAFFLES

Preheat a lightly greased Belgian waffle iron. Place 2 cups of the jar mix in a medium-sized bowl. Add the eggs, water, and oil, and mix gently with a wooden spoon or whisk until well blended. For each waffle, pour ½ cup of batter onto the hot waffle iron, and cook until golden brown. Serve hot with butter and syrup.

GRANOLACRUNCH

Enjoy this crunchy granola as a nutritious cereal
or sprinkle it on your favorite yogurt.

YIELD:
4 CUPS

**QUART-SIZE JAR
INGREDIENTS**

3 ½ cups old-
fashioned oatmeal
(not quick-cooking)

⅓ cup wheat germ

½ cup chopped
walnuts

¼ cup brown sugar

**ADDITIONAL
INGREDIENTS**

⅓ cup melted butter,
slightly cooled

⅓ cup honey

1 teaspoon
vanilla extract

½ cup chopped
dried fruit
(optional)

1. Preheat the oven to 350°F.

2. Place all of the jar ingredients except the optional dried fruit in a large bowl, and stir until well combined. Add the butter, vanilla, and honey, and mix well.

3. Spread the mixture in an even layer on an ungreased baking sheet.

4. Bake for 10 minutes, stir, and continue to bake another 10 to 15 minutes, or until lightly browned and crisp. Remove from the oven and allow to cool completely. Add dried fruit, if desired.

5. Transfer the granola to the jar or another airtight container, and store in a cool dry place.

CREATING THE JAR

3 ½ cups old-fashioned oatmeal

⅓ cup wheat germ

¼ cup brown sugar

½ cup chopped walnuts

1. Wash and thoroughly dry a 1-quart wide-mouth canning jar.

2. Layer the ingredients in the jar as shown at left, pressing each layer firmly with a flat-bottomed object, such as a tart tamper or the bottom of a narrow glass. Make the layers as level as possible.

3. Secure the lid, and decorate as desired (see page 24). Attach the instructions for making the granola found below.

Yield: 4 cups

In addition to the contents of the jar, you will need to add the following ingredients:

⅓ cup melted butter, slightly cooled

⅓ cup honey

1 teaspoon vanilla extract

½ cup chopped dried fruit (optional)

GRANOLA CRUNCH

Preheat the oven to 350°F. Place the contents of the jar in a large bowl, and stir until well combined. Add the honey, butter, and vanilla, and mix well. Spread the mixture evenly on an ungreased baking sheet. Bake for 10 minutes, stir, and continue to bake another 10 to 15 minutes, or until lightly browned and crisp. Cool completely. Add dried fruit, if desired. Transfer the granola to the jar or another airtight container, and store in a cool dry place.

OLDWORLDMUESLI

*Start the day right with this delicious homemade version
of a healthy European breakfast cereal.*

YIELD:
4 CUPS

**QUART-SIZE JAR
INGREDIENTS**

1 ½ cups corn flakes

1 cup bran flakes

½ cup quick-cooking
oatmeal

½ cup dark raisins

½ cup chopped
walnuts

1 teaspoon
cinnamon

**ADDITIONAL
INGREDIENT**

⅓ cup apple juice
concentrate

1. Preheat the oven to 300°F. Lightly grease a baking sheet and set aside.

2. Place all of the jar ingredients in a large bowl, and stir until well combined. Add the apple juice, and mix well.

3. Spread the mixture in an even layer on the baking sheet.

4. Bake 15 to 20 minutes, or until lightly browned and crisp. Allow to cool completely.

5. Transfer the muesli to the jar or another airtight container, and store in a cool dry place.

CREATING THE JAR

1 ½ cups corn flakes

1 cup bran flakes

½ cup quick-cooking oatmeal

½ cup dark raisins

½ cup chopped walnuts

1 teaspoon cinnamon

1. Wash and thoroughly dry a 1-quart wide-mouth canning jar.

2. Layer the ingredients in the jar as shown at left. With the exception of the corn flakes and bran flakes, press each layer firmly with a flat-bottomed object, such as a tart tamper or the bottom of a narrow glass. Make the layers as level as possible.

3. Secure the lid, and decorate as desired (see page 24). Attach the instructions for making the muesli found below.

Yield:
4 cups

In addition to the contents of the jar, you will need to add the following ingredient:

⅓ cup apple juice concentrate

OLD WORLD MUESLI

Preheat the oven to 300°F. Place the contents of the jar in a large bowl, and stir until well combined. Add the apple juice and mix well. Spread the mixture evenly on a lightly greased baking sheet. Bake for 15 to 20 minutes, or until lightly browned and crisp. Cool completely. Transfer the muesli to the jar or another airtight container, and store in a cool dry place.

Muffins,Scones, and**Breads**

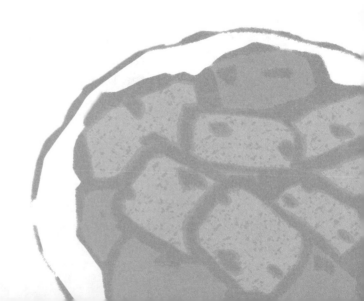

APRICOT-WALNUT MUFFINS

Flecked with juicy bits of apricots and crunchy walnuts,
these yummy muffins are blue-ribbon good!

YIELD:
12 MUFFINS

QUART-SIZE JAR INGREDIENTS

1 1/2 cups all-purpose flour

1 cup oatmeal

1/2 cup chopped dried apricots

1/3 cup chopped walnuts

1/2 cup brown sugar

2 teaspoons baking powder

1/4 teaspoon baking soda

1/4 teaspoon salt

ADDITIONAL INGREDIENTS

1 cup milk

1/4 cup melted butter, slightly cooled

1 egg, slightly beaten

1. Preheat the oven to 375°F.

2. Place all of the jar ingredients in a medium-sized bowl, and stir until well combined. Set aside.

3. Place the milk, butter, and egg in a large bowl, and cream with a whisk, fork, or an electric mixer set on low speed.

4. Add the dry ingredients to the milk mixture, and stir with a wooden spoon until just mixed. Do not overstir.

5. Spoon the batter into greased or papered muffin tins. Fill each cup about two-thirds full.

6. Bake for 20 to 25 minutes, or until a toothpick inserted into the center of a muffin comes out clean. Allow to cool for 10 minutes in the tin. Then remove the muffins and cool completely on a wire rack.

7. Serve immediately, or store in an airtight container for up to 1 week.

CREATING THE JAR

⅓ cup chopped walnuts

½ cup chopped
dried apricots

½ cup brown sugar

I cup oatmeal

¼ teaspoon salt

¼ teaspoon baking soda

2 teaspoons baking powder

I ½ cups all-purpose flour

1. Wash and thoroughly dry a 1-quart wide-mouth canning jar.

2. Layer the ingredients in the jar as shown at left, pressing firmly with a flat-bottomed object, such as a tart tamper or the bottom of a narrow glass, after each addition. Make the layers as level as possible.

3. Secure the lid, and decorate as desired (see page 24). Attach the instructions for making the muffins found below.

Yield:
12 muffins

In addition to the contents of the jar, you will need to add the following ingredients:

I cup milk

¼ cup melted butter, slightly cooled

I egg, slightly beaten

APRICOT-WALNUT MUFFINS

Preheat the oven to 375°F. In a large bowl, cream the milk, butter, and egg. Add the contents of the jar, and stir until just mixed. Do not overstir. Spoon the batter into greased or papered muffin tins, filling each cup two-thirds full. Bake for 20 to 25 minutes, or until a toothpick inserted into the center of a muffin comes out clean. Cool 10 minutes in the tin, remove, and cool completely. Serve immediately, or store in an airtight container for up to 1 week.

GINGERSPICEMUFFINS

Moist and flavorful, these heavenly muffins
are absolutely delicious.

YIELD:
12 MUFFINS

PINT-SIZE JAR INGREDIENTS

1¾ cups all-purpose flour

½ cup sugar

2 teaspoons baking powder

½ teaspoon salt

I teaspoon cinnamon

½ teaspoon nutmeg

¼ teaspoon ground ginger

¼ teaspoon ground cloves

ADDITIONAL INGREDIENTS

I cup milk

¼ cup melted butter, slightly cooled

I egg

I teaspoon vanilla extract

1. Preheat the oven to 400°F.

2. Place all of the jar ingredients in a medium-sized bowl, and stir until well combined. Set aside.

3. Place the milk, butter, egg, and vanilla in a large bowl, and cream with a whisk, fork, or an electric mixer set on low speed.

4. Add the dry ingredients to the milk mixture, and stir with a wooden spoon until just mixed. Do not overstir.

5. Spoon the batter into greased or papered muffin tins. Fill each cup about two-thirds full.

6. Bake for 15 to 20 minutes, or until a toothpick inserted into the center of a muffin comes out clean. Allow to cool for 10 minutes in the tin. Then remove the muffins and cool completely on a wire rack.

7. Serve immediately, or store in an airtight container for up to 1 week.

CREATING THE JAR

1 ¾ cups all-purpose flour

½ cup sugar

2 teaspoons baking powder

½ teaspoon salt

1 teaspoon cinnamon

½ teaspoon nutmeg

¼ teaspoon ground ginger

¼ teaspoon ground cloves

1. Wash and thoroughly dry a 1-pint wide-mouth canning jar.

2. Layer the ingredients in the jar as shown at left, pressing firmly with a flat-bottomed object, such as a tart tamper or the bottom of a narrow glass, after each addition. Make the layers as level as possible.

3. Secure the lid, and decorate as desired (see page 24). Attach the instructions for making the muffins found below.

Yield:
12 muffins

In addition to the contents of the jar, you will need to add the following ingredients:

1 cup milk

¼ cup melted butter, slightly cooled

1 egg, slightly beaten

1 teaspoon vanilla extract

GINGER SPICE MUFFINS

Preheat the oven to 400°F. In a large bowl, cream the milk, butter, egg, and vanilla. Add the contents of the jar, and stir until just mixed. Do not overstir. Spoon the batter into greased or papered muffin tins, filling each cup two-thirds full. Bake for 15 to 20 minutes, or until a toothpick inserted into the center of a muffin comes out clean. Cool 10 minutes in the tin, remove, and cool completely. Serve immediately, or store in an airtight container for up to 1 week.

GOLDENPECANMUFFINS

These luscious gems are great with coffee.
You won't be able to stop at just one.

YIELD:
12 MUFFINS

PINT-SIZE JAR
INGREDIENTS

1 ½ cups all-purpose
flour

½ cup sugar

½ cup chopped
pecans

2 teaspoons
baking powder

½ teaspoon
cinnamon

½ teaspoon salt

ADDITIONAL
INGREDIENTS

½ cup milk

¼ cup vegetable oil

1 egg, slightly beaten

1. Preheat the oven to 400°F.

2. Place all of the jar ingredients in a medium-sized bowl, and stir until well combined. Set aside.

3. Place the milk, oil, and egg in a large bowl, and blend well with a whisk, fork, or an electric mixer set on low speed.

4. Add the dry ingredients to the milk mixture, and stir with a wooden spoon until just mixed. Do not overstir.

5. Spoon the batter into greased or papered muffin tins. Fill each cup about two-thirds full.

6. Bake for 15 to 18 minutes or until a toothpick inserted into the center of a muffin comes out clean. Allow to cool for 10 minutes in the tin. Then remove the muffins and cool completely on a wire rack.

7. Serve immediately, or store in an airtight container for up to 1 week.

CREATINGTHEJAR

½ cup chopped pecans

1 ½ cups all-purpose flour

½ cup sugar

2 teaspoons baking powder

½ teaspoon cinnamon

½ teaspoon salt

1. Wash and thoroughly dry a 1-pint wide-mouth canning jar.

2. Layer the ingredients in the jar as shown at left, pressing firmly with a flat-bottomed object, such as a tart tamper or the bottom of a narrow glass, after each addition. Make the layers as level as possible.

3. Secure the lid, and decorate as desired (see page 24). Attach the instructions for making the muffins found below.

Yield: 12 muffins

In addition to the contents of the jar, you will need to add the following ingredients:

½ cup milk

¼ cup vegetable oil

1 egg, slightly beaten

GOLDEN PECAN MUFFINS

Preheat the oven to 400°F. In a large bowl, blend the milk, oil, and egg. Add the contents of the jar, and stir until just mixed. Do not overstir. Spoon the batter into greased or papered muffin tins, filling each cup two-thirds full. Bake for 15 to 18 minutes, or until a toothpick inserted into the center of a muffin comes out clean. Cool 10 minutes in the tin, remove, and cool completely. Serve immediately, or store in an airtight container for up to 1 week.

RAISINBRANMUFFINS

Start the day with one of these fiber-rich muffins.

YIELD:
12 MUFFINS

QUART-SIZE JAR INGREDIENTS

1 1/2 cups bran flakes

1 1/4 cups self-rising flour

1 cup dark raisins

1/2 cup sugar

ADDITIONAL INGREDIENTS

1/2 cup milk

1/2 cup melted butter, slightly cooled

1 egg, slightly beaten

1. Preheat the oven to 400°F.

2. Place all of the jar ingredients in a medium-sized bowl, and stir until well combined. Set aside.

3. Place the milk, butter, and egg in a large bowl, and cream with a whisk, fork, or an electric mixer set on low speed.

4. Add the dry ingredients to the milk mixture, and stir with a wooden spoon until just mixed. Do not overstir.

5. Spoon the batter into greased or papered muffin tins. Fill each cup about two-thirds full.

6. Bake for 15 to 18 minutes, or until a toothpick inserted into the center of a muffin comes out clean. Allow to cool for 10 minutes in the tin. Then remove the muffins and cool completely on a wire rack.

7. Serve immediately, or store in an airtight container for up to 1 week.

CREATINGTHEJAR

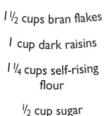

1½ cups bran flakes

1 cup dark raisins

1¼ cups self-rising flour

½ cup sugar

1. Wash and thoroughly dry a 1-quart wide-mouth canning jar.

2. Layer the ingredients in the jar as shown at left, pressing firmly with a flat-bottomed object, such as a tart tamper or the bottom of a narrow glass, after each addition. Make the layers as level as possible.

3. Secure the lid, and decorate as desired (see page 24). Attach the instructions for making the muffins found below.

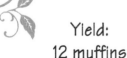

Yield: 12 muffins

In addition to the contents of the jar, you will need to add the following ingredients:

½ cup milk

½ cup melted butter, slightly cooled

1 egg, slightly beaten

RAISIN BRAN MUFFINS

Preheat the oven to 400°F. In a large bowl, cream the milk, butter, and egg. Add the contents of the jar, and stir until just mixed. Do not overstir. Spoon the batter into greased or papered muffin tins, filling each cup two-thirds full. Bake for 15 to 18 minutes, or until a toothpick inserted into the center of a muffin comes out clean. Cool 10 minutes in the tin, remove, and cool completely. Serve immediately, or store in an airtight container for up to 1 week.

BLUEBERRYSCONES

Similar to sweet biscuits, these blueberry scones
are considered special treats in my home.

YIELD:
10 TO 12 SCONES

QUART-SIZE JAR
INGREDIENTS

2 cups all-purpose
flour

1 cup dried
blueberries

⅓ cup sugar

¼ cup nonfat
dry milk

2 teaspoons
baking powder

1 teaspoon dried
lemon peel

¼ teaspoon salt

ADDITIONAL
INGREDIENTS

⅓ cup vegetable
shortening

1 egg, beaten

¼ cup cold water

1. Preheat the oven to 400°F.

2. Place all of the jar ingredients in a large bowl, and stir until well combined.

3. Using a pastry blender or two knives, cut the shortening into the mixture until it resembles coarse crumbs. Stir in the egg and enough of the water to just moisten the mixture. Form into a ball.

4. Turn the dough onto a lightly floured surface. With floured hands, gently knead the dough 12 to 15 times. Do not over knead. Pat the dough into a ½ inch-thick circle.

5. Using a floured 2½-inch biscuit or cookie cutter, cut the dough into rounds. Place the rounds 1 inch apart on an ungreased baking sheet.

6. Bake for 12 to 15 minutes, or until lightly browned. Transfer the scones to wire racks and cool slightly. Serve warm.

CREATINGTHEJAR

¼ teaspoon salt

1 teaspoon dried lemon peel

2 teaspoons baking powder

¼ cup nonfat dry milk

1 cup dried blueberries

⅓ cup sugar

2 cups all-purpose flour

1. Wash and thoroughly dry a 1-quart wide-mouth canning jar.

2. Layer the ingredients in the jar as shown at left, pressing firmly with a flat-bottomed object, such as a tart tamper or the bottom of a narrow glass, after each addition. Make the layers as level as possible.

3. Secure the lid, and decorate as desired (see page 24). Attach the instructions for making the scones found below.

Yield:
10 to 12 scones

In addition to the contents of the jar, you will need to add the following ingredients:

⅓ cup vegetable shortening

1 egg, beaten

¼ cup cold water

BLUEBERRY SCONES

Preheat the oven to 400°F. Place the contents of the jar in a large bowl and stir. Cut in the shortening until the mixture resembles coarse crumbs. Stir in the egg and enough water to just moisten, and form into a ball. Turn the dough onto a lightly floured surface, gently knead 12 to 15 times, then pat into a ½-inch-thick circle. Using a 2½-inch biscuit or cookie cutter, cut rounds into the dough. Place the rounds 1 inch apart on an ungreased baking sheet. Bake 12 to 15 minutes, or until lightly browned. Serve warm.

CINNAMON-RAISIN SCONES

These cinnamon-flavored, raisin-filled scones
can be described in one word—heavenly.

YIELD:
10 TO 12 SCONES

QUART-SIZE JAR INGREDIENTS

2 cups all-purpose flour

⅓ cup sugar

¼ cup nonfat dry milk

2 teaspoons baking powder

1 teaspoon cinnamon

¼ teaspoon salt

1 cup dark raisins

ADDITIONAL INGREDIENTS

⅓ cup vegetable shortening

1 egg, beaten

¼ cup cold water

1. Preheat the oven to 400°F.

2. Place all of the jar ingredients in a large bowl, and stir until well combined.

3. Using a pastry blender or two knives, cut the shortening into the mixture until it resembles coarse crumbs. Stir in the egg and enough of the water to just moisten the mixture. Form into a ball.

4. Turn the dough onto a lightly floured surface. With floured hands, gently knead the dough 12 to 15 times. Do not over knead. Pat the dough into a ½ inch-thick circle.

5. Using a floured 2½-inch biscuit or cookie cutter, cut the dough into rounds. Place the rounds 1 inch apart on an ungreased baking sheet.

6. Bake for 12 to 15 minutes, or until lightly browned. Transfer the scones to wire racks and cool slightly. Serve warm.

CREATING THE JAR

¼ teaspoon salt

I teaspoon cinnamon

2 teaspoons baking powder

¼ cup nonfat dry milk

I cup dark raisins

⅓ cup sugar

2 cups all-purpose flour

1. Wash and thoroughly dry a 1-quart wide-mouth canning jar.

2. Layer the ingredients in the jar as shown at left, pressing firmly with a flat-bottomed object, such as a tart tamper or the bottom of a narrow glass, after each addition. Make the layers as level as possible.

3. Secure the lid, and decorate as desired (see page 24). Attach the instructions for making the scones found below.

Yield:
10 to 12 scones

In addition to the contents of the jar, you will need to add the following ingredients:

⅓ cup vegetable shortening

I egg, beaten

¼ cup cold water

CINNAMON-RAISIN SCONES

Preheat the oven to 400°F. Place the contents of the jar in a large bowl and stir. Cut in the shortening until the mixture resembles coarse crumbs. Stir in the egg and enough water to just moisten, and form into a ball. Turn the dough onto a lightly floured surface, gently knead 12 to 15 times, then pat into a ½-inch-thick circle. Using a 2½-inch biscuit or cookie cutter, cut rounds into the dough. Place the rounds 1 inch apart on an ungreased baking sheet. Bake 12 to 15 minutes, or until lightly browned. Serve warm.

BUTTERPECANBREAD

Brown sugar and cinnamon add just the right sweetness
to this rich, buttery bread.

YIELD:
9-INCH LOAF

**QUART-SIZE JAR
INGREDIENTS**

2 1/4 cups all-purpose
flour

1 cup chopped
pecans

1 cup brown sugar

2 teaspoons
baking powder

1/2 teaspoon
baking soda

1/2 teaspoon
cinnamon

1/2 teaspoon salt

1/4 teaspoon nutmeg

**ADDITIONAL
INGREDIENTS**

1 cup buttermilk

2 tablespoons butter,
softened

1 egg, slightly beaten

1. Preheat the oven to 350°F. Generously grease a 9-x-5-inch loaf pan and set aside.

2. Place all of the jar ingredients in a medium-sized bowl, and stir until well combined. Set aside.

3. Place the buttermilk, butter, and egg in a large bowl, and cream with a whisk, fork, or an electric mixer set on low speed.

4. Add the dry ingredients to the milk mixture, and stir with a wooden spoon until just mixed. Do not overstir. Pour the batter into the prepared loaf pan.

5. Bake for 50 to 55 minutes, or until a toothpick inserted into the center of the loaf comes out clean. Cool for 10 minutes in the pan. Then remove the bread and cool completely on a wire rack

6. Serve immediately, or store in an airtight container for up to 1 week.

CREATING THE JAR

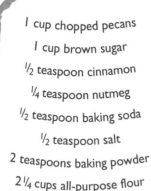

1 cup chopped pecans

1 cup brown sugar

1/2 teaspoon cinnamon

1/4 teaspoon nutmeg

1/2 teaspoon baking soda

1/2 teaspoon salt

2 teaspoons baking powder

2 1/4 cups all-purpose flour

1. Wash and thoroughly dry a 1-quart wide-mouth canning jar.

2. Layer the ingredients in the jar as shown at left, pressing firmly with a flat-bottomed object, such as a tart tamper or the bottom of a narrow glass, after each addition. Make the layers as level as possible.

3. Secure the lid, and decorate as desired (see page 24). Attach the instructions for making the bread found below.

Yield:
9-inch loaf

In addition to the contents of the jar, you will need to add the following ingredients:

1 cup buttermilk

2 tablespoons butter, softened

1 egg, slightly beaten

BUTTER PECAN BREAD

Preheat the oven to 350°F. In a large bowl, cream the buttermilk, butter, and egg. Add the contents of the jar, and stir until just mixed. Do not overstir. Pour the batter into a greased 9-x-5-inch loaf pan. Bake for 50 to 55 minutes, or until a toothpick inserted into the center of the loaf comes out clean. Cool 10 minutes in the pan, then remove the bread and cool completely on a wire rack. Serve immediately, or store in an airtight container for up to 1 week.

CHOCOLATECHIP BANANABREAD

If you've never combined the flavor of bananas and chocolate, now is the time. You'll want to make this wonderful bread on special occasions.

YIELD:
9-INCH LOAF

QUART-SIZE JAR INGREDIENTS

1 cup chocolate chips

$\frac{1}{2}$ cup coarsely chopped dried bananas

$\frac{1}{2}$ cup sugar

1 teaspoon baking powder

$\frac{1}{4}$ teaspoon salt

2 $\frac{1}{2}$ cups biscuit mix

ADDITIONAL INGREDIENTS

1 $\frac{1}{4}$ cups buttermilk

$\frac{1}{2}$ cup butter, softened

2 eggs, slightly beaten

1 teaspoon vanilla extract

1. Preheat the oven to 350°F. Generously grease a 9-x-5-inch loaf pan and set aside.

2. Place all of the jar ingredients in a medium-sized bowl, and stir until well combined. Set aside.

3. Place the buttermilk, butter, eggs, and vanilla in a large bowl, and cream with a whisk, fork, or an electric mixer set on low speed.

4. Add the dry ingredients to the milk mixture, and stir with a wooden spoon until just mixed. Do not overstir. Pour the batter into the prepared loaf pan.

5. Bake for 50 to 55 minutes, or until a toothpick inserted into the center of the loaf comes out clean. Cool for 10 minutes in the pan. Then remove the bread and cool completely on a wire rack.

6. Serve immediately, or store in an airtight container for up to 1 week.

CREATINGTHEJAR

I cup chocolate chips

½ cup coarsely chopped dried bananas

½ cup sugar

I teaspoon baking powder

¼ teaspoon salt

2½ cups biscuit mix

1. Wash and thoroughly dry a 1-quart wide-mouth canning jar.

2. Layer the ingredients in the jar as shown at left, pressing firmly with a flat-bottomed object, such as a tart tamper or the bottom of a narrow glass, after each addition. Make the layers as level as possible.

3. Secure the lid, and decorate as desired (see page 24). Attach the instructions for making the bread found below.

Yield: 9-inch loaf

In addition to the contents of the jar, you will need to add the following ingredients:

I ¼ cups buttermilk

½ cup butter, softened

2 eggs, slightly beaten

I teaspoon vanilla extract

CHOCOLATE CHIP BANANA BREAD

Preheat the oven to 350°F. In a large bowl, cream the buttermilk, butter, eggs, and vanilla extract. Add the contents of the jar, and stir until just mixed. Do not overstir. Pour the batter into a greased 9-x-5-inch loaf pan. Bake for 50 to 55 minutes, or until a toothpick inserted into the center of the loaf comes out clean. Cool 10 minutes in the pan, then remove the bread and cool completely on a wire rack. Serve immediately, or store in an airtight container for up to 1 week.

CHOCOLATECHIP RAISINBREAD

The tantalizing aroma and delectable taste of this
chocolate and raisin-sweetened bread makes it hard to resist.

YIELD:
9-INCH LOAF

QUART-SIZE JAR INGREDIENTS

I cup chocolate chips

¹/₂ cup raisins

¹/₂ cup chopped walnuts

¹/₂ cup sugar

I teaspoon baking powder

¹/₄ teaspoon salt

2¹/₂ cups biscuit mix

ADDITIONAL INGREDIENTS

1¹/₄ cups buttermilk

¹/₂ cup butter, softened

2 eggs, slightly beaten

I teaspoon vanilla extract

1. Preheat the oven to 350°F. Generously grease a 9-x-5-inch loaf pan and set aside.

2. Place all of the jar ingredients in a medium-sized bowl, and stir until well combined. Set aside.

3. Place the buttermilk, butter, eggs, and vanilla in a large bowl, and cream with a whisk, fork, or an electric mixer set on low speed.

4. Add the dry ingredients to the milk mixture, and stir with a wooden spoon until just mixed. Do not overstir. Pour the batter into the prepared loaf pan.

5. Bake for 50 to 55 minutes, or until a toothpick inserted into the center of the loaf comes out clean. Cool for 10 minutes in the pan. Then remove the bread and cool completely on a wire rack.

6. Serve immediately, or store in an airtight container for up to 1 week.

I cup chocolate chips

½ cup raisins

½ cup chopped walnuts

½ cup sugar

1 teaspoon baking powder

¼ teaspoon salt

2½ cups biscuit mix

CREATING THE JAR

1. Wash and thoroughly dry a 1-quart wide-mouth canning jar.

2. Layer the ingredients in the jar as shown at left, pressing firmly with a flat-bottomed object, such as a tart tamper or the bottom of a narrow glass, after each addition. Make the layers as level as possible.

3. Secure the lid, and decorate as desired (see page 24). Attach the instructions for making the bread found below.

Yield:
9-inch loaf

In addition to the contents of the jar, you will need to add the following ingredients:

1¼ cups buttermilk

½ cup butter, softened

2 eggs, slightly beaten

1 teaspoon vanilla extract

CHOCOLATE CHIP RAISIN BREAD

Preheat the oven to 350°F. In a large bowl, cream the buttermilk, butter, eggs, and vanilla extract. Add the contents of the jar, and stir until just mixed. Do not overstir. Pour the batter into a greased 9-x-5-inch loaf pan. Bake for 50 to 55 minutes, or until a toothpick inserted into the center of the loaf comes out clean. Cool 10 minutes in the pan, then remove the bread and cool completely on a wire rack. Serve immediately, or store in an airtight container for up to 1 week.

GOLDENCORNBREAD

Topped with butter and honey, this cornbread is a little taste of heaven.
Enjoy it alone, with a cup of hot tea, or alongside
a steaming bowl of chili.

YIELD:
8 SERVINGS

**PINT-SIZE JAR
INGREDIENTS**

1 ¼ cups biscuit mix

½ cup cornmeal

½ cup sugar

1 tablespoon
baking powder

**ADDITIONAL
INGREDIENTS**

1 cup milk

½ cup melted butter,
slightly cooled

2 eggs, slightly beaten

1. Preheat the oven to 350°F. Generously grease a 9-inch-round cake pan, and set aside.

2. Place all of the jar ingredients in a medium-sized bowl, and stir until well combined. Set aside.

3. Place the milk, butter, and eggs in a large bowl, and cream with a whisk, fork, or an electric mixer set on low speed.

4. Add the dry ingredients to the milk mixture, and stir with a wooden spoon until just mixed. Do not overstir. Pour the batter into the prepared pan.

5. Bake for 30 to 35 minutes, or until a toothpick inserted into the center of the cornbread comes out clean. Cool completely before cutting into wedges.

6. Serve immediately, or store in an airtight container for up to 1 week.

CREATINGTHEJAR

1 ¼ cups biscuit mix

½ cup cornmeal

½ cup sugar

1 tablespoon baking powder

1. Wash and thoroughly dry a 1-pint wide-mouth canning jar.

2. Layer the ingredients in the jar as shown at left, pressing firmly with a flat-bottomed object, such as a tart tamper or the bottom of a narrow glass, after each addition. Make the layers as level as possible.

3. Secure the lid, and decorate as desired (see page 24). Attach the instructions for making the cornbread found below.

Yield:
8 servings

In addition to the contents of the jar, you will need to add the following ingredients:

1 cup milk

½ cup melted butter, slightly cooled

2 eggs, slightly beaten

GOLDEN CORNBREAD

Preheat the oven to 350°F. In a large bowl, cream the milk, butter, and eggs. Add the contents of the jar, and stir until just mixed. Do not overstir. Pour the batter into a greased 9-inch-round cake pan. Bake for 30 to 35 minutes, or until a toothpick inserted into the center of the cornbread comes out clean. Cool completely before cutting into wedges. Serve immediately, or store in an airtight container for up to 1 week.

MOM'SBLUEBERRYBREAD

If you're a fan of blueberries, you'll love this bread.
Try a slice topped with country fresh butter.

YIELD:
9-INCH LOAF

QUART-SIZE JAR INGREDIENTS

2 1/2 cups biscuit mix

1 cup chopped walnuts

1/2 cup dried blueberries

1/2 cup sugar

1 teaspoon baking powder

1/4 teaspoon salt

ADDITIONAL INGREDIENTS

1 1/4 cups buttermilk

1/2 cup butter, softened

1 teaspoon vanilla extract

2 eggs, slightly beaten

1. Preheat the oven to 350°F. Generously grease a 9-x-5-inch loaf pan and set aside.

2. Place all of the jar ingredients in a medium-sized bowl, and stir until well combined. Set aside.

3. Place the buttermilk, butter, vanilla, and eggs in a large bowl and cream with a whisk, fork, or an electric mixer set on low speed.

4. Add the dry ingredients to the milk mixture, and stir with a wooden spoon until just mixed. Do not overstir. Pour the batter into the prepared loaf pan.

5. Bake for 50 to 55 minutes or until a toothpick inserted into the center of the loaf comes out clean. Cool for 10 minutes. Then remove the bread from the pan and cool completely on a wire rack.

6. Serve immediately, or store in an airtight container for up to 1 week.

I cup chopped walnuts

½ cup dried blueberries

½ cup sugar

I teaspoon baking powder

¼ teaspoon salt

2½ cups biscuit mix

CREATINGTHEJAR

1. Wash and thoroughly dry a 1-quart wide-mouth canning jar.

2. Layer the ingredients in the jar as shown at left, pressing firmly with a flat-bottomed object, such as a tart tamper or the bottom of a narrow glass, after each addition. Make the layers as level as possible.

3. Secure the lid, and decorate as desired (see page 24). Attach the instructions for making the bread found below.

Yield: 9-inch loaf

In addition to the contents of the jar, you will need to add the following ingredients:

1¼ cups buttermilk

½ cup butter, softened

1 teaspoon vanilla extract

2 eggs, slightly beaten

MOM'S BLUEBERRY BREAD

Preheat the oven to 350°F. In a large bowl, cream the buttermilk, butter, vanilla, and eggs. Add the contents of the jar, and stir until just mixed. Do not overstir. Pour the batter into a greased 9-x-5-inch loaf pan. Bake for 50 to 55 minutes, or until a toothpick inserted into the center of the loaf comes out clean. Cool 10 minutes in the pan, then remove the bread and cool completely on a wire rack. Serve immediately, or store in an airtight container for up to 1 week.

NUTTYCRANBERRYBREAD

*Here's the perfect bread to serve
with Thanksgiving dinner.*

YIELD:
9-INCH LOAF

**QUART-SIZE JAR
INGREDIENTS**

2 ½ cups biscuit mix

1 cup chopped
walnuts

½ cup dried
cranberries

½ cup sugar

1 teaspoon
baking powder

¼ teaspoon salt

**ADDITIONAL
INGREDIENTS**

1 ¼ cups buttermilk

½ cup butter,
softened

1 teaspoon
vanilla extract

2 eggs, slightly beaten

1. Preheat the oven to 350°F. Generously grease a 9-x-5-inch loaf pan and set aside.

2. Place all of the jar ingredients in a medium-sized bowl, and stir until well combined. Set aside.

3. Place the buttermilk, butter, vanilla, and eggs in a large bowl, and cream with a whisk, fork, or an electric mixer set on low speed.

4. Add the dry ingredients to the milk mixture, and stir with a wooden spoon until just mixed. Do not overstir. Pour the batter into the prepared loaf pan.

5. Bake for 50 to 55 minutes, or until a toothpick inserted into the center of the loaf comes out clean. Cool for 10 minutes. Then remove the bread and cool completely on a wire rack.

6. Serve immediately, or store in an airtight container for up to 1 week.

I cup chopped walnuts

½ cup dried cranberries

½ cup sugar

I teaspoon baking powder

¼ teaspoon salt

2½ cups biscuit mix

CREATING THE JAR

1. Wash and thoroughly dry a 1-quart wide-mouth canning jar.

2. Layer the ingredients in the jar as shown at left, pressing firmly with a flat-bottomed object, such as a tart tamper or the bottom of a narrow glass, after each addition. Make the layers as level as possible.

3. Secure the lid, and decorate as desired (see page 24). Attach the instructions for making the bread found below.

Yield:
9-inch loaf

In addition to the contents of the jar, you will need to add the following ingredients:

1¼ cups buttermilk

½ cup butter, softened

1 teaspoon vanilla extract

2 eggs, slightly beaten

NUTTY CRANBERRY BREAD

Preheat the oven to 350°F. In a large bowl, cream the buttermilk, butter, vanilla, and eggs. Add the contents of the jar, and stir until just mixed. Do not overstir. Pour the batter into a greased 9-x-5-inch loaf pan. Bake for 50 to 55 minutes, or until a toothpick inserted into the center of the loaf comes out clean. Cool 10 minutes in the pan, then remove the bread and cool completely on a wire rack. Serve immediately, or store in an airtight container for up to 1 week.

CookiesandCakes

CHOCOLATEBISCOTTI

Cocoa powder gives this twice-baked treat its rich chocolate taste.
Great with a mug of coffee, cup of tea, or glass of ice cold milk.

YIELD:
ABOUT 36 COOKIES

PINT-SIZE JAR INGREDIENTS

1 1/3 cups all-purpose flour

2/3 cup sugar

1/2 cup unsweetened cocoa powder

1 1/2 teaspoons baking powder

1/2 teaspoon baking soda

ADDITIONAL INGREDIENTS

3 tablespoons butter, softened

2 eggs

1/2 teaspoon vanilla extract

1/2 cup chopped almonds

1. Preheat the oven to 350°F. Grease a baking sheet and set aside.

2. Place all of the jar ingredients in a medium-sized bowl, and stir until well combined. Set aside.

3. Place the butter, eggs, and vanilla in a large bowl, and cream with an electric mixer set on low speed.

4. Add the dry ingredients to the butter mixture, and continue blending until well combined. Stir in the almonds. Gather the mixture into a ball, and knead to form a moist cookie dough.

5. Divide the dough in half. If the dough is sticky, flour your hands before shaping each half into a 12-inch log. Flatten the logs slightly until they are about 1/2 inch high and 1 1/2 inches wide. Place them about 3 inches apart on the prepared baking sheet.

6. Bake for 20 minutes, or until partially baked and beginning to dry. Remove the pan from the oven, and carefully transfer the logs to a cutting board. Allow to cool for 5 minutes, or until warm to the touch.

7. Using a serrated knife, cut the warm logs diagonally into 1/2-inch-thick slices. Arrange the slices cut side down on the baking sheet, and return to the oven for about 15 minutes to dry slightly. Transfer to wire racks and cool completely.

8. Serve immediately, or store in an airtight container for up to 2 weeks.

CREATINGTHEJAR

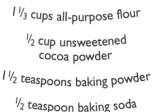

1 ⅓ cups all-purpose flour

½ cup unsweetened cocoa powder

1 ½ teaspoons baking powder

½ teaspoon baking soda

⅔ cup sugar

1. Wash and thoroughly dry a 1-pint wide-mouth canning jar.

2. Layer the ingredients in the jar as shown at left, pressing firmly with a flat-bottomed object, such as a tart tamper or the bottom of a narrow glass, after each addition. Make the layers as level as possible. For best results, when adding the flour, add a little at a time, firmly tamping after each addition.

3. Secure the lid, and decorate as desired (see page 24). Attach the instructions for making the cookies found below.

Yield: About 36 cookies

In addition to the contents of the jar, you will need to add the following ingredients:

3 tablespoons butter, softened

2 eggs

½ teaspoon vanilla extract

½ cup chopped almonds

CHOCOLATE BISCOTTI

Preheat the oven to 350°F. In a large bowl, cream the butter, eggs, and vanilla with an electric mixer set on low speed. Add the contents of the jar, and mix until well combined. Stir in the almonds. Gather the mixture into a ball and knead to form a moist cookie dough. Divide in half. Shape each half into a 12-inch log, ½ inch high and 1½ inches wide. Place on greased baking sheet, and bake for 20 minutes. Remove from oven, and cool for 5 minutes. Cut logs diagonally into ½-inch slices, and arrange on baking sheet cut side down. Return to oven for 15 minutes to dry slightly. Cool completely. Serve immediately, or store in an airtight container for up to 2 weeks.

OATMEAL RAISIN COOKIES

This all-time favorite cookie combines the chewy goodness of oatmeal
with the natural sweetness of raisins. An irresistible classic!

YIELD:
ABOUT 30 COOKIES

QUART-SIZE JAR INGREDIENTS

2 cups quick-cooking oatmeal

1 cup all-purpose flour

3/4 cup packed brown sugar

3/4 cup dark raisins

1/2 cup sugar

1 teaspoon baking soda

1 teaspoon ground cinnamon

1/2 teaspoon ground nutmeg

1/2 teaspoon salt

ADDITIONAL INGREDIENTS

3/4 cup butter, softened

1 egg

1 teaspoon vanilla extract

1. Preheat the oven to 350°F.

2. Place all of the jar ingredients in a medium-sized bowl, and stir until well combined. Set aside.

3. Place the butter, egg, and vanilla in a large bowl, and cream with a whisk, fork, or an electric mixer set on low speed.

4. Add the dry ingredients to the butter mixture, and stir with a wooden spoon until well combined.

5. Drop the dough by heaping teaspoonfuls onto an ungreased baking sheet, spacing the cookies about 2 inches apart to allow for spreading.

6. Bake for 11 to 13 minutes, or until the edges are light brown in color. Allow to cool for 5 minutes on the baking sheet. Then transfer to wire racks and cool completely.

7. Serve immediately, or store in an airtight container for up to 2 weeks.

CREATING THE JAR

½ cup sugar

¾ cup packed brown sugar

2 cups quick-cooking oatmeal

¾ cup dark raisins

½ teaspoon salt

1 teaspoon baking soda

½ teaspoon ground nutmeg

1 teaspoon ground cinnamon

1 cup all-purpose flour

1. Wash and thoroughly dry a 1-quart wide-mouth canning jar.

2. Layer the ingredients in the jar as shown at left, pressing firmly with a flat-bottomed object, such as a tart tamper or the bottom of a narrow glass, after each addition. Make the layers as level as possible.

3. Secure the lid, and decorate as desired (see page 24). Attach the instructions for making the cookies found below.

Yield:
About 30 cookies

In addition to the contents of the jar, you will need to add the following ingredients:

¾ cup butter, softened

1 egg

1 teaspoon vanilla extract

OATMEAL RAISIN COOKIES

Preheat the oven to 350°F. In a large bowl, cream the butter, egg, and vanilla. Add the contents of the jar, and stir until well mixed. Drop the dough by heaping teaspoons onto an ungreased baking sheet, spacing the cookies about 2 inches apart. Bake 11 to 13 minutes, or until the edges are light brown in color. Allow to cool for 5 minutes on the baking sheet, then transfer to wire racks and cool completely. Serve immediately, or store in an airtight container for up to 2 weeks.

SCOTTISHSHORTBREAD

This flaky shortbread is sweet and buttery rich.
Try some during your next coffee break.

YIELD:
16 COOKIES

PINT-SIZE JAR
INGREDIENTS

1 ½ cups all-purpose
flour

¾ cup powdered
sugar

¼ teaspoon salt

ADDITIONAL
INGREDIENT

1 cup butter,
softened

1. Preheat the oven to 300°F.

2. Place all of the jar ingredients in a medium-sized bowl, and stir until well combined. Add the butter, and mix thoroughly with a wooden spoon or an electric mixer set at low speed to form a thick batter.

3. Spread the batter evenly in an ungreased 8-x-8-inch baking pan, and bake for 55 to 60 minutes, or until light brown in color.

4. Allow the shortbread to cool completely in the pan before cutting into 16 cookies (2-inch squares).

5. Serve immediately, or store in an airtight container for up to 10 days.

CREATING THE JAR

1 ½ cups all-purpose flour

¾ cup powdered sugar

¼ teaspoon salt

1. Wash and thoroughly dry a 1-pint wide-mouth canning jar.

2. Layer the ingredients in the jar as shown at left, pressing firmly with a flat-bottomed object, such as a tart tamper or the bottom of a narrow glass, after each addition. Make the layers as level as possible.

3. Secure the lid, and decorate as desired (see page 24). Attach the instructions for making the shortbread found below.

Yield:
16 cookies

In addition to the contents of the jar, you will need to add the following ingredient:

1 cup butter, softened

SCOTTISH SHORTBREAD

Preheat oven to 300°F. Place the contents of the jar in a medium-sized bowl. Add the butter, and mix thoroughly with a wooden spoon or an electric mixer set at low speed to form a thick batter. Spread the batter evenly in an ungreased 8-x-8-inch baking pan, and bake for 55 to 60 minutes, or until light brown in color. Cool the shortbread completely in the pan before cutting into 2-inch squares. Serve immediately, or store in an airtight container for up to 10 days.

TOFFEECHIPCOOKIES

If you like the buttery crunch of toffee, these delicious cookies
won't disappoint. You'll want to keep your cookie jar filled with them.

YIELD:
ABOUT 36 COOKIES

QUART-SIZE JAR
INGREDIENTS

I cup biscuit mix

²/₃ cup toffee chips

¹/₂ cup chopped
toasted pecans,
cooled

¹/₂ cup brown sugar

ADDITIONAL
INGREDIENTS

¹/₂ cup butter,
softened

I egg

I teaspoon
vanilla extract

1. Preheat the oven to 375°F.

2. Place all of the jar ingredients in a medium-sized bowl, and stir until well combined. Set aside.

3. Place the butter, egg, and vanilla in a large bowl, and cream with a whisk, fork, or an electric mixer set on low speed.

4. Add the dry ingredients to the butter mixture, and stir with a wooden spoon until well combined.

5. Drop the dough by heaping teaspoonfuls onto an ungreased baking sheet, spacing the cookies about 2 inches apart to allow for spreading.

6. Bake for 10 to 12 minutes, or until the edges are light brown in color. Allow to cool for 5 minutes on the baking sheet. Then transfer to wire racks and cool completely.

7. Serve immediately, or store in an airtight container for up to 2 weeks.

CREATING THE JAR

2/3 cup toffee chips

1/2 cup chopped toasted pecans, cooled

1/2 cup brown sugar

1 cup biscuit mix

1. Wash and thoroughly dry a 1-quart wide-mouth canning jar.

2. Layer the ingredients in the jar as shown at left, pressing firmly with a flat-bottomed object, such as a tart tamper or the bottom of a narrow glass, after each addition. Make the layers as level as possible.

3. Secure the lid, and decorate as desired (see page 24). Attach the instructions for making the cookies found below.

Yield: About 36 cookies

In addition to the contents of the jar, you will need to add the following ingredients:

1/2 cup butter, softened

1 egg

1 teaspoon vanilla extract

TOFFEE CHIP COOKIES

Preheat the oven to 375°F. In a large bowl, cream the butter, egg, and vanilla. Add the contents of the jar, and stir until well mixed. Drop the dough by heaping teaspoonfuls onto an ungreased baking sheet, spacing the cookies about 2 inches apart. Bake for 10 to 12 minutes, or until the edges are light brown in color. Allow to cool for 5 minutes on the baking sheet, then transfer to wire racks and cool completely. Serve immediately, or store in an airtight container for up to 2 weeks.

YUMMYBARS

The double Ms in this recipe title stand for M&Ms candies—
a key ingredient in these delicious gems.

YIELD:
16 COOKIES

QUART-SIZE JAR
INGREDIENTS

2 cups biscuit mix

1 cup brown sugar

1/2 cup quick-cooking
oatmeal

1/2 cup miniature
candy-coated
chocolate pieces,
such as M&M's
Baking Bits

ADDITIONAL
INGREDIENTS

1/2 cup butter,
softened

1 egg

1 teaspoon
vanilla extract

1. Preheat the oven to 350°F. Grease an 8-x-8-inch baking pan and set aside.

2. Place all of the jar ingredients in a medium-sized bowl, and stir until well combined. Set aside.

3. Place the butter, egg, and vanilla in a large bowl, and cream with a whisk, fork, or an electric mixer set on low speed.

4. Add the dry ingredients to the butter mixture, and stir with a wooden spoon until well combined.

5. Spread the batter evenly in the prepared pan, and bake for 25 to 30 minutes, or until a toothpick inserted into the center comes out clean. Allow to cool completely in the pan before cutting into 16 cookies (2-inch squares).

6. Serve immediately, or store in an airtight container for up to 1 week.

CREATING THE JAR

½ cup quick-cooking oatmeal

½ cup miniature candy-coated chocolate pieces

½ cup brown sugar

1 cup biscuit mix

½ cup brown sugar

1 cup biscuit mix

1. Wash and thoroughly dry a 1-quart wide-mouth canning jar.

2. Layer the ingredients in the jar as shown at left, pressing firmly with a flat-bottomed object, such as a tart tamper or the bottom of a narrow glass, after each addition. Make the layers as level as possible.

3. Secure the lid, and decorate as desired (see page 24). Attach the instructions for making the bars found below.

Yield: 16 cookies

In addition to the contents of the jar, you will need to add the following ingredients:

½ cup butter, softened

1 egg

1 teaspoon vanilla extract

YUMMY BARS

Preheat the oven to 350°F. In a large bowl, cream the butter, egg, and vanilla. Add the contents of the jar, and stir until well mixed. Spread the batter evenly in a greased 8-x-8-inch baking pan, and bake for 25 to 30 minutes, or until a toothpick inserted into the center comes out clean. Cool completely in the pan before cutting into 2-inch squares. Serve immediately, or store in an airtight container for up to 1 week.

"GOOD-DOG"TREATS

*Just for fun, I've added this recipe, which makes a unique gift for
dog owners. My dog, Belle, will "sit" for these treats every time!*

YIELD:
ABOUT 48 TREATS

**QUART-SIZE JAR
INGREDIENTS**

3 cups whole
wheat flour

I cup nonfat
dry milk

3 tablespoons dry
chicken gravy mix

3 tablespoons
brown sugar

**ADDITIONAL
INGREDIENTS**

I egg

²/₃ cup vegetable oil

I cup warm water

1. Preheat the oven to 300°F.

2. Place all of the jar ingredients in a large bowl, and stir until well combined. Add the egg, oil, and water. Stir the ingredients together to form a soft dough.

3. Turn the dough onto a floured surface, and knead for 3 minutes. Using a floured rolling pin, roll out the dough to a 12-x-12-inch square that is ¼ inch thick. Cut the dough into 1½-x-2-inch pieces, or cut out shapes with your favorite cookie cutters. (Bone-shaped cutters are available at many pet supply stores.) Place about 1 inch apart on an ungreased baking sheet.

4. Bake for 20 minutes, then turn the cookies over. Continue to bake another 10 minutes, or until lightly browned on both sides. Allow to cool completely on the baking sheet.

5. Store in an airtight container.

CREATINGTHEJAR

3 cups whole wheat flour

1 cup nonfat dry milk

3 tablespoons dry chicken gravy mix

3 tablespoons brown sugar

1. Wash and thoroughly dry a 1-quart wide-mouth canning jar.

2. Layer the ingredients in the jar as shown at left, pressing firmly with a flat-bottomed object, such as a tart tamper or the bottom of a narrow glass, after each addition. Make the layers as level as possible.

3. Secure the lid, and decorate as desired (see page 24). Attach the instructions for making the dog treats found below.

Yield:
About 48 treats

In addition to the contents of the jar, you will need to add the following ingredients:

1 egg

⅔ cup vegetable oil

1 cup warm water

"GOOD-DOG" TREATS

Preheat the oven to 300°F. Place the contents of the jar in a large bowl. Add the egg, oil, and water, and stir well to form a soft dough. Turn onto a floured surface, knead for 3 minutes, then roll into a ¼ inch thick 12-inch square. Cut into 1½-x-2-inch pieces, or cut into shapes with a cookie cutter. (Bone-shaped cutters are sold at many pet supply stores.) Place about 1 inch apart on an ungreased baking sheet. Bake for 20 minutes, turn over, and continue to bake another 10 minutes, or until lightly browned on both sides. Cool completely before storing in an airtight container.

CARROTCAKE

This moist, delicious cake will have everyone asking for seconds.

YIELD:
12 SERVINGS

QUART-SIZE JAR
INGREDIENTS

3 cups all-purpose
flour

1²/₃ cups sugar

2 teaspoons
baking soda

2 teaspoons pumpkin
pie spice

ADDITIONAL
INGREDIENTS

3 eggs, slightly beaten

1¹/₂ cups vegetable oil

2 teaspoons
vanilla extract

3 cups grated carrots

8-ounce can crushed
pineapple, drained

1. Preheat the oven to 350°F. Generously grease a 9-x-13-inch baking pan and set aside.

2. Place all of the jar ingredients in a medium-sized bowl, and stir until well combined. Set aside.

3. Place the eggs, oil, and vanilla in a large bowl, and blend well with a fork or an electric mixer set on low speed.

4. Add the dry ingredients to the egg mixture, and continue to blend until well combined. Stir in the carrots and pineapple. Pour the batter into the prepared baking pan.

5. Bake for 33 to 38 minutes, or until a toothpick inserted into the center of the cake comes out clean. Cool completely before adding frosting or dusting with powdered sugar.

6. Serve immediately, or store in an airtight container for up to 1 week.

CREATING THE JAR

2 teaspoons baking soda

2 teaspoons
pumpkin pie spice

3 cups all-purpose flour

1 2/3 cups sugar

1. Wash and thoroughly dry a 1-quart wide-mouth canning jar.

2. Layer the ingredients in the jar as shown at left, pressing firmly with a flat-bottomed object, such as a tart tamper or the bottom of a narrow glass, after each addition. Make the layers as level as possible. For best results, when adding the flour, add a little at a time, firmly tamping after each addition.

3. Secure the lid, and decorate as desired (see page 24). Attach the instructions for making the cake found below.

Yield:
12 servings

In addition to the contents of the jar, you will need to add the following ingredients:

3 eggs, slightly beaten

1 1/2 cups vegetable oil

2 teaspoons vanilla extract

3 cups grated carrots

8-ounce can crushed pineapple, drained

Carrot Cake

Preheat the oven to 350°F. Place the eggs, oil, and vanilla in a large bowl, and blend well with an electric mixer set on low speed. Add the contents of the jar and continue to blend until well combined. Stir in the carrots and pineapple. Pour the batter into a greased 9-x-13-inch baking pan, and bake for 33 to 38 minutes, or until a toothpick inserted into the center of the cake comes out clean. Cool completely before adding frosting or dusting with powdered sugar. Serve immediately, or store in an airtight container for up to 1 week.

FUNNELCAKES

*Now you can bring the county fair into your very own kitchen
with these delicious, easy-to-make funnel cakes.*

YIELD:
4 FUNNEL CAKES

**PINT-SIZE JAR
INGREDIENTS**

2 cups all-purpose
flour

1 teaspoon
baking soda

1/2 teaspoon salt

**ADDITIONAL
INGREDIENTS**

2 eggs, lightly beaten

1 1/2 cups milk

Vegetable oil
for frying

1. Place the eggs in a large bowl. Add the milk, while gently stirring with a whisk or fork until well combined.

2. Add the jar ingredients to the egg mixture, and stir to form a well-blended, smooth batter. Set aside.

3. Heat 1 1/2 inches of oil in a large skillet set over medium-high heat. To determine if the oil is hot enough, drop a small dollop of batter into the skillet. If it fries briskly and browns in 30 seconds, the oil is ready.

4. Pour 1/4 cup of batter into a funnel while holding your finger over the tip (for best results, the tip should be at least 1/2 inch in diameter). Position the funnel a few inches above the skillet, remove your finger from the tip, and let the batter flow into the hot oil in a spiral-shaped design. Repeat with the remaining batter

5. Fry for 1 to 2 minutes or until the bottoms are golden brown. Carefully turn the cakes over and cook another minute. Transfer to paper towels to absorb any oil.

6. Serve immediately as is or topped with powdered sugar, cinnamon sugar, or your favorite fruit pie filling.

2 cups all-purpose flour

1 teaspoon baking soda

1/2 teaspoon salt

CREATINGTHEJAR

1. Wash and thoroughly dry a 1-pint wide-mouth canning jar.

2. Combine the ingredients in the jar shown at left, and transfer the mixture to the canning jar.

3. Secure the lid, and decorate as desired (see page 24). Attach the instructions for making the funnel cakes found below.

Yield:
4 funnel cakes

In addition to the contents of the jar, you will need to add the following ingredients:

2 eggs, lightly beaten

1 1/2 cups milk

Vegetable oil for frying

FUNNEL CAKES

In a large bowl, combine the eggs and milk. Add the jar ingredients, stir until smooth, and set aside. Heat 1 1/2 inches of oil in a large skillet set over medium-high heat. Pour 1/4 cup of batter into a funnel while holding your finger over the tip. Position funnel over the skillet, remove finger from tip, and let the batter flow into the hot oil in a spiral-shaped design. Repeat with remaining batter. Fry 1 to 2 minutes, or until the bottoms are golden brown. Turn cakes over, and cook another minute. Drain on paper towels. Serve plain, or topped with powdered sugar, cinnamon sugar, or fruit pie filling.

LEMONPOPPYSEEDCAKE

A warm glaze crowns this moist and zesty lemon cake.

YIELD:
12 SERVINGS

QUART-SIZE JAR INGREDIENTS

3 cups all-purpose flour

1 1/2 cups sugar

1/4 cup poppy seeds

1 1/2 teaspoons baking powder

ADDITIONAL INGREDIENTS

1 cup vegetable oil

1/3 cup milk

6 eggs

1 teaspoon vanilla extract

1 teaspoon lemon extract

1/2 teaspoon lemon zest

FOR GLAZE:

1/2 cup sugar

1/2 cup lemon juice

1. Preheat the oven to 350°F. Generously grease a 12-cup (10-inch) bundt pan and set aside.

2. Place the butter, milk, eggs, vanilla, lemon extract, and lemon zest in a large bowl, and cream with an electric mixer set on low speed. Add the jar ingredients and continue mixing until well combined. Pour the batter into the prepared pan.

3. Bake for 45 to 50 minutes, or until a toothpick inserted into the center of the cake comes out clean. Remove from the oven and allow to cool for 5 minutes in the pan.

4. Prepare the glaze by stirring the sugar and lemon juice together in a small saucepan, and bring to a boil over medium-high heat. Boil for 3 minutes.

5. Remove the cake from the pan, and place it on a serving plate. Spoon the glaze over the warm cake, letting it drip down the sides. Cool completely.

6. Serve immediately, or store in an airtight container for up to 1 week.

CREATINGTHEJAR

1½ cups sugar

3 cups all-purpose flour

1½ teaspoons baking powder

¼ cup poppy seeds

1. Wash and thoroughly dry a 1-quart wide-mouth canning jar.

2. In a large bowl, combine all of the ingredients listed in the jar shown at left, pressing firmly with a flat-bottomed object, such as a tart tamper or the bottom of a narrow glass, after each addition. For best results, when adding the flour, add a little at a time, firmly tamping after each addition.

3. Secure the lid, and decorate as desired (see page 24). Attach the instructions for making the cake found below.

Yield: 12 servings

In addition to the contents of the jar, you will need to add the following ingredients:

1 cup vegetable oil

⅓ cup milk

6 eggs

1 teaspoon vanilla extract

1 teaspoon lemon extract

½ teaspoon lemon zest

FOR GLAZE:

½ cup sugar

½ cup lemon juice

LEMON POPPY SEED CAKE

Preheat the oven to 350°F. In a large bowl, cream the butter, milk, eggs, vanilla, lemon extract, and lemon zest with an electric mixer set on low speed. Add the jar ingredients, and continue mixing until well combined. Pour batter into a greased 12-cup (10-inch) bundt pan, and bake for 45 to 50 minutes, or until a toothpick inserted into the center comes out clean. Remove from oven and cool for 5 minutes in the pan. Prepare the glaze by boiling the sugar and lemon juice in a small pan for 3 minutes. Remove the warm cake from the pan, place on a serving plate, and spoon the glaze on top. Cool completely. Serve immediately, or store in an airtight container for up to 1 week.

LOW-FATSPICECAKE

*Using applesauce instead of oil in this recipe creates a delicious
guilt-free cake that any weight watcher will enjoy.*

YIELD:
12 SERVINGS

**QUART-SIZE JAR
INGREDIENTS**

2 cups whole
wheat flour

I cup sugar

³/₄ cup packed
brown sugar

¹/₃ cup nonfat
dry milk

¹/₃ cup dark raisins

I ¹/₄ teaspoons
baking powder

I teaspoon
baking soda

I teaspoon salt

¹/₂ teaspoon
ground cinnamon

¹/₂ teaspoon
ground cloves

**ADDITIONAL
INGREDIENTS**

3 eggs

2 cups applesauce

¹/₂ cup chopped
walnuts (optional)

1. Preheat the oven to 325°F. Generously grease a 12-cup (10-inch) bundt pan and set aside.

2. Place all of the jar ingredients in a medium-sized bowl, and stir until well combined. Set aside.

3. Place the eggs and applesauce in a large bowl, and blend well with an electric mixer set on low speed.

4. Add the dry ingredients to the egg mixture, and continue mixing for 2 minutes. Stir in walnuts, if desired. Pour the batter into the prepared pan.

5. Bake for 45 to 50 minutes, or until a toothpick inserted into the center of the cake comes out clean. Cool for 10 minutes in the pan, then remove the cake and cool completely on a wire rack. Dust lightly with powdered sugar, if desired.

6. Serve immediately, or store in an airtight container for up to 1 week.

CREATING THE JAR

½ teaspoon ground cloves

½ teaspoon ground cinnamon

I teaspoon baking soda

I teaspoon salt

1¼ teaspoons baking powder

2 cups whole wheat flour

I cup sugar

¾ cup brown sugar

⅓ cup nonfat dry milk

⅓ cup dark raisins

1. Wash and thoroughly dry a 1-quart wide-mouth canning jar.

2. Layer the ingredients in the jar as shown at left, pressing firmly with a flat-bottomed object, such as a tart tamper or the bottom of a narrow glass, after each addition. Make the layers as level as possible.

3. Secure the lid, and decorate as desired (see page 24). Attach the instructions for making the cake found below.

Yield: 12 servings

In addition to the contents of the jar, you will need to add the following ingredients:

3 eggs

2 cups applesauce

½ cup chopped walnuts (optional)

LOW FAT SPICE CAKE

Preheat the oven to 325°F. Place the eggs and applesauce in a large bowl, and blend with an electric mixer set on low speed. Add the contents of the jar, and continue to blend until well-combined. Stir in walnuts, if desired. Pour the batter into a greased 12-cup (10-inch) bundt pan, and bake for 45 to 50 minutes, or until a toothpick inserted into the center of the cake comes out clean. Cool for 10 minutes in the pan, then remove the cake and cool completely on a wire rack. Dust lightly with powdered sugar, if desired. Serve immediately or store in an airtight container for up to 1 week.

MYFAVORITECHOCOLATECAKE

Chocolate lovers everywhere will know why this moist,
rich chocolaty cake is my personal favorite!

YIELD:
9 SERVINGS

QUART-SIZE JAR INGREDIENTS

2 cups flour

²/₃ cup unsweetened cocoa powder

³/₄ teaspoon salt

1 ¹/₂ teaspoons baking powder

1 ¹/₃ cups sugar

ADDITIONAL INGREDIENTS

³/₄ cup vegetable oil

2 teaspoons white vinegar

1 teaspoon vanilla extract

2 cups water

1. Preheat the oven to 350°F. Generously grease an 8-x-8-inch baking pan and set aside.

2. Place all of the jar ingredients in a large bowl, and stir until well combined. Add the oil, vinegar, vanilla, and water, and blend with an electric mixer on low speed for 2 minutes. Pour the batter into the prepared baking pan.

3. Bake for 40 to 50 minutes, or until a toothpick inserted into the center of the cake comes out clean. Cool for 10 minutes in the pan. Then remove the cake and cool completely on a wire rack. Sprinkle with powdered sugar or frost with your favorite icing, if desired.

4. Serve immediately, or store in an airtight container for up to 1 week.

CREATING THE JAR

2 cups flour

²/₃ cup unsweetened cocoa powder

¾ teaspoon salt

1 ½ teaspoons baking powder

1 ⅓ cups sugar

1. Wash and thoroughly dry a 1-quart wide-mouth canning jar.

2. Layer the ingredients in the jar as shown at left, pressing firmly with a flat-bottomed object, such as a tart tamper or the bottom of a narrow glass, after each addition. Make the layers as level as possible.

3. Secure the lid, and decorate as desired (see page 24). Attach the instructions for making the cake found below.

Yield: 9 servings

In addition to the contents of the jar, you will need to add the following ingredients:

¾ cup vegetable oil

2 teaspoons white vinegar

1 teaspoon vanilla extract

2 cups water

MY FAVORITE CHOCOLATE CAKE

Preheat the oven to 350°F. Place the contents of the jar in a large bowl and stir until well combined. Add the oil, vinegar, vanilla, and water, and blend with an electric mixer on low speed for 2 minutes. Pour the batter into a greased 8-x-8-inch baking pan, and bake for 40 to 50 minutes, or until a toothpick inserted into the center of the cake comes out clean. Cool for 10 minutes in the pan, then remove the cake and cool completely on a wire rack. Sprinkle with powdered sugar or frost with your favorite icing, if desired. Serve immediately, or store in an airtight container for up to 1 week.

PEACHCOBBLER

Although this recipe calls for peaches, any "cobbler type" fruit will do.
Apples, peaches, blueberries, and cherries are among my favorites.

YIELD:
9 SERVINGS

PINT-SIZE JAR
INGREDIENTS

I cup all-purpose
flour

I cup sugar

I teaspoon
baking powder

ADDITIONAL
INGREDIENTS

4 ¹⁄₂ cups peeled
sliced peaches

¹⁄₄ cup sugar

¹⁄₄ cup orange juice

I teaspoon
cinnamon

I egg, slightly beaten

¹⁄₂ cup melted butter,
slightly cooled

1. Preheat the oven to 375°F.

2. Place the peaches, sugar, orange juice, and cinnamon in a large bowl. Stir to mix well, and set aside.

3. Place the egg, butter, and jar ingredients in a medium bowl. Blend well with a fork, whisk, or wooden spoon to form a smooth batter.

4. Pour the fruit mixture into an ungreased 8-x-8-inch baking pan. Drop heaping tablespoons of the batter on top.

5. Bake for 45 to 50 minutes, or until the top is golden brown. Allow to cool for 20 minutes.

6. Serve immediately, or store in an airtight container for up to 1 week.

CREATING THE JAR

I cup all-purpose flour

I cup sugar

I teaspoon baking powder

1. Wash and thoroughly dry a 1-pint wide-mouth canning jar.

2. Layer the ingredients in the jar as shown at left, pressing firmly with a flat-bottomed object, such as a tart tamper or the bottom of a narrow glass, after each addition. Make the layers as level as possible.

3. Secure the lid, and decorate as desired (see page 24). Attach the instructions for making the cobbler found below.

Yield: 9 servings

In addition to the contents of the jar, you will need to add the following ingredients:

4 ½ cups peeled sliced peaches

¼ cup sugar

¼ cup orange juice

I teaspoon cinnamon

I egg, slightly beaten

½ cup melted butter, slightly cooled

PEACH COBBLER

Preheat the oven to 375°F. In a large bowl, combine the peaches, sugar, orange juice, and cinnamon, and set aside. In a medium bowl, blend the egg, butter, and jar ingredients to form a smooth batter. Pour the peach mixture into an ungreased 8-x-8-inch baking pan. Drop heaping tablespoons of the batter on top. Bake for 45 to 50 minutes, or until the top is golden brown. Allow to cool for 20 minutes. Serve immediately, or store in an airtight container for up to 1 week.

SPICEDAPPLECAKE

Loaded with fresh apples and plump raisins,
this luscious cake is difficult to resist.

YIELD:
12 SERVINGS

QUART-SIZE JAR INGREDIENTS

3 cups all-purpose flour

1 $\frac{1}{2}$ cups sugar

1 $\frac{1}{2}$ teaspoons baking soda

1 $\frac{1}{2}$ teaspoons ground cinnamon

$\frac{1}{4}$ teaspoon ground nutmeg

$\frac{1}{2}$ cup raisins

ADDITIONAL INGREDIENTS

3 eggs, slightly beaten

1 $\frac{1}{2}$ cups vegetable oil

1 teaspoon vanilla extract

3 cups chopped apples

1 cup chopped pecans (optional)

1. Preheat the oven to 350°F. Generously grease a 12-cup (10-inch) bundt pan and set aside.

2. Place all of the jar ingredients in a medium-sized bowl, and stir until well combined. Set aside.

3. Place the eggs, oil, and vanilla in a large bowl, and blend well with an electric mixer on low speed for 2 minutes.

4. Add the dry ingredients to the egg mixture, and continue to blend until well combined. Stir in the apples. If using pecans, stir them into the batter. Pour the batter into the prepared pan.

5. Bake for 60 to 75 minutes, or until a toothpick inserted into the center of the cake comes out clean. Cool for 10 minutes in the pan, then remove the cake and cool completely on a wire rack.

6. Serve immediately, or store in an airtight container for up to 1 week.

CREATING THE JAR

½ cup raisins

¼ teaspoon ground nutmeg

1½ teaspoons ground cinnamon

1½ teaspoons baking soda

1½ cups sugar

3 cups all-purpose flour

1. Wash and thoroughly dry a 1-quart wide-mouth canning jar.

2. Layer the ingredients in the jar as shown at left, pressing firmly with a flat-bottomed object, such as a tart tamper or the bottom of a narrow glass, after each addition. Make the layers as level as possible.

3. Secure the lid, and decorate as desired (see page 24). Attach the instructions for making the cake found below.

Yield:
12 servings

In addition to the contents of the jar, you will need to add the following ingredients:

3 eggs, slightly beaten

1½ cups vegetable oil

1 teaspoon vanilla extract

3 cups chopped apples

1 cup chopped pecans (optional)

SPICED APPLE CAKE

Preheat the oven to 350°F. In a large bowl, blend the eggs, oil, and vanilla with an electric mixer on low speed. Add the contents of the jar, and continue mixing until well combined. Stir in the apples and pecans, if desired. Pour the batter into a greased 12-cup (10-inch) bundt pan, and bake for 60 to 75 minutes, or until a toothpick inserted into the center of the cake comes out clean. Cool for 10 minutes in the pan, then remove the cake and cool completely on a wire rack. Serve immediately, or store in an airtight container for up to 1 week.

Soupsand**Stews**

BARLEYRICESTEW

YIELD:
6 (1 CUP) SERVINGS

*This thick heartwarming stew is perfect fare
on a cold winter day.*

**PINT-SIZE JAR
INGREDIENTS***

¹/₂ cup barley

¹/₂ cup white rice

¹/₂ cup dried
minced onion

¹/₃ cup imitation
bacon bits

¹/₄ cup chicken
bouillon granules

1 tablespoon
brown sugar

1 teaspoon
dried basil

1 teaspoon
dried oregano

¹/₂ teaspoon
black pepper

¹/₂ teaspoon dried
minced garlic

¹/₂ teaspoon
celery salt

**ADDITIONAL
INGREDIENT**

7 cups water

* For quart jar, double
the ingredient amounts.

1. Place all of the jar ingredients in a medium-sized pot. Add the water and stir well.

2. Bring to a boil over medium-high heat. Reduce the heat to low, stir, and cover. Stirring occasionally, simmer for 1 hour, or until the rice and barley are tender and the stew is thick. Serve hot.

3. Refrigerate any leftover stew in an airtight container for up to 1 week.

CREATING THE JAR

½ cup barley

⅓ cup imitation bacon bits

1 tablespoon brown sugar

1 teaspoon dried basil

1 teaspoon dried oregano

½ teaspoon black pepper

½ teaspoon dried minced garlic

½ teaspoon celery salt

¼ cup chicken bouillon granules

½ cup white rice

½ cup dried minced onion

For quart jar, double ingredient amounts.

1. Wash and thoroughly dry a 1-pint wide-mouth canning jar.

2. Layer the ingredients in the jar shown at left, pressing firmly with a flat-bottomed object, such as a tart tamper or the bottom of a narrow glass, after each addition. Make the layers as level as possible.

3. Secure the lid, and decorate as desired (see page 24). Attach the instructions for making the stew found below.

Pint-Jar Yield: 6 (1 cup) servings

In addition to the contents of the jar, you will need to add the following ingredient:

7 cups water

For quart jar, double the ingredient amount.

BARLEY RICE STEW

Combine the water and contents of the jar in a medium-sized pot, and bring to a boil over medium-high heat. Reduce the heat to low, stir, and cover. Stirring occasionally, simmer for 1 hour, or until the barley is tender and the stew is thick. Serve hot. Refrigerate any leftovers in an airtight container for up to 1 week.

BEEFYBEANSOUP

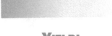

QUART-SIZE JAR INGREDIENTS*

1 cup green split peas

1 cup lentils

1 cup pearl barley

½ cup elbow macaroni

½ cup dried onion flakes

2 tablespoons dried parsley

2 teaspoons celery flakes

1 teaspoon ground pepper

ADDITIONAL INGREDIENTS

1 pound ground beef

12 cups (3 quarts) beef broth

* For pint jar, use half of the ingredient amounts.

Packed with fiber, this hearty soup is thick and satisfying.

1. Coat a large pot or Dutch oven with cooking spray, and preheat over medium-high heat. Add the beef, and cook, stirring constantly for about 4 minutes, or until no pink remains. Remove any excess fat.

2. Add the broth and all of the jar ingredients except the macaroni to the pot. Bring to a boil over medium-high heat. Reduce the heat to low, cover, and simmer for 30 minutes while stirring occasionally.

3. Add the macaroni, and continue to simmer another 10 minutes, or until the peas are tender and the macaroni is cooked. Serve hot.

4. Refrigerate any leftover soup in an airtight container for up to 1 week.

CREATING THE JAR

½ cup elbow macaroni

1 teaspoon ground pepper

2 tablespoons dried parsley

2 teaspoons celery flakes

½ cup dried onion flakes

1 cup pearl barley

1 cup lentils

1 cup green split peas

For pint jar, use half of the ingredient amounts.

1. Wash and thoroughly dry a 1-quart wide-mouth canning jar.

2. Place the macaroni in a plastic sandwich bag.

3. Layer the ingredients in the jar as shown at left, pressing firmly with a flat-bottomed object, such as a tart tamper or the bottom of a narrow glass, after each addition. Make the layers as level as possible.

4. Secure the lid, and decorate as desired (see page 24). Attach the instructions for making the soup found below.

Quart-Jar Yield: 15 (1 cup) servings

In addition to the contents of the jar, you will need to add the following ingredients:

1 pound ground beef

12 cups (3 quarts) beef broth

For pint jar, use half of the ingredient amounts.

BEEFY BEAN SOUP

In a large pot or Dutch oven, brown the ground beef and drain. Add the broth and all of the jar ingredients except the macaroni. Bring to a boil over medium-high heat. Reduce the heat to low, cover, and simmer for 30 minutes while stirring occasionally. Add the macaroni, and continue to simmer another 10 minutes, or until the peas are tender and the macaroni is cooked. Serve hot. Refrigerate any leftovers in an airtight container for up to 1 week.

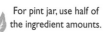

BEEFYCHILISOUP

*Each satisfying spoonful of this savory soup is thick with beef
and beans. The perfect choice on a cold winter's day.*

YIELD:
8 (1 CUP) SERVINGS

**PINT-SIZE JAR
INGREDIENTS***

1/2 cup red
kidney beans

1/2 cup navy beans

1/2 cup black beans

1/3 cup dried
minced onion

2 tablespoons
chili powder

2 tablespoons
dried cilantro

2 teaspoons cumin

1 teaspoon sugar

1 teaspoon salt

1/2 teaspoon
garlic powder

**ADDITIONAL
INGREDIENTS**

2 pounds
ground beef

6 cups water

3 cans (14 ounces
each) tomato juice

* For quart jar, double
the ingredient amounts.

1. Place the kidney, navy, and black beans in a medium-sized bowl or pot. Cover with 6 cups boiling water, cover, and soak 8 hours or overnight.

2. Coat a medium-sized pot or Dutch oven with cooking spray, and preheat over medium-high heat. Add the beef, and cook, stirring constantly for 4 minutes, or until no pink remains. Remove any excess fat, and set aside.

3. Drain and rinse the soaked beans, and add them to the pot along with 6 cups fresh water and all of the jar ingredients. Bring to a boil over medium-high heat. Reduce the heat to low, cover, and simmer for 1½ to 2 hours, or until the beans are tender. Stir the soup occasionally as it simmers.

4. Add the tomato juice and return to a boil. Reduce the heat to low, cover, and simmer another 15 minutes. Serve immediately.

5. Refrigerate any leftover soup in an airtight container for up to 1 week.

CREATING THE JAR

Premixed seasoning packet:

½ teaspoon garlic powder
1 teaspoon salt
2 teaspoons ground cumin
2 tablespoons dried cilantro
1 teaspoon sugar
2 tablespoons chili powder
⅓ cup dried minced onion

½ cup black beans

½ cup navy beans

½ cup red kidney beans

For quart jar, double ingredient amounts.

1. Wash and thoroughly dry a 1-pint wide-mouth canning jar.

2. Place all of the seasonings in the jar shown at left in a plastic sandwich bag.

3. Layer the ingredients in the jar as shown at left, pressing firmly with a flat-bottomed object, such as a tart tamper or the bottom of a narrow glass, after each addition. Make the layers as level as possible.

3. Secure the lid, and decorate as desired (see page 24). Attach the instructions for making the soup found below.

Pint-Jar Yield: 8 (1 cup) servings

In addition to the contents of the jar, you will need to add the following ingredients:

2 pounds ground beef

6 cups water

3 cans (14 ounces each) tomato juice

For quart jar, double the ingredient amounts.

BEEFY CHILI SOUP

Place the kidney, navy, and black beans in a medium-sized bowl, cover with 6 cups boiling water, and soak 8 hours or overnight. In a medium-sized pot, brown the ground beef. Drain and rinse the soaked beans, and add them to the pot with 6 cups fresh water and contents of the seasoning packet. Bring to a boil, then reduce the heat to low. Cover and simmer for 1½ to 2 hours, or until the beans are tender. Stir the soup occasionally as it simmers. Add the tomato juice and return to a boil. Reduce the heat, cover, and simmer another 15 minutes. Serve hot. Refrigerate any leftovers in an airtight container for up to 1 week.

BEEFYMACSOUP

This easy-to-prepare soup is both filling and delicious—
a real crowd pleaser.

YIELD:
6 (1 CUP) SERVINGS

PINT-SIZE JAR INGREDIENTS*

½ cup green split peas

¼ cup lentils

2 envelopes (1 ounce each) onion soup mix

¾ cup macaroni, such as elbows or small shells

ADDITIONAL INGREDIENTS

1 pound ground beef

7 cups water

14.5-ounce can stewed tomatoes

* For quart jar, double the ingredient amounts.

1. Coat a medium-sized pot or Dutch oven with cooking spray, and preheat over medium-high heat. Add the beef, and cook, stirring constantly for 4 minutes, or until no pink remains. Remove any excess fat, and set aside.

2. Add the water, tomatoes, and all of the jar ingredients except the macaroni to the pot. Bring to a boil over medium-high heat. Reduce the heat to low, cover, and simmer for 50 minutes while stirring occasionally.

3. Stir in the macaroni. Continue to simmer another 10 minutes, or until the macaroni is cooked. Serve hot.

4. Refrigerate any leftover soup in an airtight container for up to 1 week.

CREATING THE JAR

¾ cup macaroni, such as elbows or small shells

½ cup green split peas

¼ cup lentils

Contents of 2 envelopes (1 ounce each) onion soup mix

For quart jar, double the ingredient amounts.

1. Wash and thoroughly dry a 1-pint wide-mouth canning jar.

2. Place the macaroni in a plastic sandwich bag.

3. Layer the ingredients in the jar as shown at left, pressing firmly with a flat-bottomed object, such as a tart tamper or the bottom of a narrow glass, after each addition. Make the layers as level as possible.

4. Secure the lid, and decorate as desired (see page 24). Attach the instructions for making the soup found below.

Pint-Jar Yield: 6 (1 cup) servings

In addition to the contents of the jar, you will need to add the following ingredients:

1 pound ground beef

7 cups water

14.5-ounce can stewed tomatoes

For quart jar, double the ingredient amounts.

BEEFY MAC SOUP

In a medium-sized pot or Dutch oven, brown the ground beef and drain. Add the water, tomatoes, and all of the jar ingredients except the macaroni to the pot. Bring to a boil over medium-high heat. Reduce the heat to low, cover, and simmer for 50 minutes while stirring occasionally. Add the macaroni, and continue to simmer another 10 minutes, or until the macaroni is cooked. Serve hot. Refrigerate any leftovers in an airtight container for up to 1 week.

DEWING'S HEARTY VEGETABLE BEEF STEW

QUART-SIZE JAR INGREDIENTS*

3/4 cup long grain rice

1/2 cup pearl barley

1/2 cup green split peas

1/2 cup lentils

1/2 cup dried minced onion

1/2 cup beef bouillon granules

2 teaspoons Italian seasoning

1 cup alphabet macaroni

ADDITIONAL INGREDIENTS

1 pound ground beef

12 cups (3 quarts) water

2 cans (16 ounces each) stewed tomatoes

* For pint jar, use half of the ingredient amounts.

My best friend, Dewing, created this thick nutritious stew, which is always a big hit.

1. Coat a large pot or Dutch oven with cooking spray, and preheat over medium-high heat. Add the beef, and cook, stirring constantly for 4 minutes, or until no pink remains. Remove any excess fat, and set aside.

2. Add the water, tomatoes, and all of the jar ingredients except the macaroni to the pot. Bring to a boil over medium-high heat. Reduce the heat to low, cover, and simmer for 40 to 45 minutes, or until the peas and lentils are soft and the barley and rice are tender.

3. Stir in the macaroni. Simmer another 10 minutes, or until the macaroni is cooked. Serve immediately.

4. Refrigerate any leftover stew in an airtight container for up to 1 week.

CREATING THE JAR

½ cup green split peas

½ cup pearl barley

½ cup lentils

½ cup dried minced onion

¾ cup long grain rice

½ cup beef bouillon granules

2 teaspoons Italian seasoning

1 cup alphabet macaroni

*For pint jar, use half of
the ingredient amounts.*

1. Wash and thoroughly dry a 1-quart wide-mouth canning jar.

2. Place the macaroni in a plastic sandwich bag.

3. Layer the ingredients in the jar as shown at left, pressing firmly with a flat-bottomed object, such as a tart tamper or the bottom of a narrow glass, after each addition. Make the layers as level as possible.

3. Secure the lid, and decorate as desired (see page 24). Attach the instructions for making the stew found below.

Quart-Jar Yield:
15 (1 cup) servings

In addition to the contents of the jar, you will need to add the following ingredients:

1 pound ground beef

12 cups (3 quarts) water

2 cans (16 ounces each) stewed tomatoes

*For pint jar, use half of
the ingredient amounts.*

DEWING'S HEARTY VEGETABLE BEEF STEW

In a large pot or Dutch oven, brown the ground beef and drain. Add the water, tomatoes, and all of the jar ingredients except the macaroni. Bring to a boil over medium-high heat, Reduce the heat to low, cover, and simmer for 40 to 45 minutes, or until the peas and lentils are soft and the barley and rice are tender. Stir in the macaroni. Simmer another 10 minutes, or until the macaroni is cooked. Serve hot. Refrigerate any leftovers in an airtight container for up to 1 week.

GOBBLE-UPTURKEY NOODLESOUP

YIELD:
10 (1 CUP) SERVINGS

QUART-SIZE JAR INGREDIENTS*

3 cups egg noodles

1 tablespoon chicken bouillon granules

2 teaspoons black pepper

2 teaspoons salt

1 teaspoon poultry seasoning

1/4 teaspoon celery seeds

1/4 teaspoon garlic powder

1 bay leaf

ADDITIONAL INGREDIENTS

10 cups water

2 carrots, sliced

2 celery stalks, diced

1/2 cup minced onion

3 cups chopped cooked turkey

* For pint jar, use half of the ingredient amounts.

Looking for a delicious way to use up that leftover Thanksgiving turkey? Look no further than this delicious noodle-rich soup.

1. Place all of the jar ingredients except the noodles in a large pot. Add the water, carrots, celery, and onion, and mix well.

2. Bring to a boil over medium-high heat. Reduce the heat to low, cover, and simmer for 15 minutes.

3. Add the noodles and turkey, and continue to simmer another 5 to 8 minutes, or until the noodles are cooked. Remove and discard the bay leaf. Serve hot.

4. Refrigerate any leftover soup in an airtight container for up to 1 week.

CREATINGTHEJAR

Premixed
seasoning packet:

I bay leaf

1/2 tablespoon chicken bouillon granules

1/2 teaspoon black pepper

1/4 teaspoon dried thyme

1/8 teaspoon garlic powder

1/8 teaspoon celery seeds

3 cups egg noodles

For pint jar, use half of
the ingredient amounts.

1. Wash and thoroughly dry a 1-quart wide-mouth canning jar.

2. Place all of the seasonings in the jar shown at left in a plastic sandwich bag.

3. Add the noodles to the jar, and place the seasoning packet on top.

4. Secure the lid, and decorate as desired (see page 24). Attach the instructions for making the soup found below.

Quart-Jar Yield:
10 (1 cup) servings

In addition to the contents of
the jar, you will need to add
the following ingredients:

10 cups water

2 carrots, sliced

2 celery stalks, diced

1/2 cup minced onion

3 cups chopped cooked turkey

For pint jar, use half of
the ingredient amounts.

GOBBLE-UP TURKEY NOODLE SOUP

Empty the contents of the seasoning packet into a large pot. Add the water, carrots, celery, and onion, and mix well. Bring to a boil over medium-high heat. Reduce the heat to low, cover, and simmer for 15 minutes. Add the noodles and turkey, and continue to simmer another 5 to 8 minutes, or until the noodles are cooked. Remove and discard the bay leaf before serving. Refrigerate any leftovers in an airtight container for up to 1 week.

HEARTYPOTATO-BEANSOUP

*This creamy bean soup is a favorite in my home.
I often serve it for dinner along with thick slices of ham
and warm buttermilk biscuits.*

YIELD:
12 (1 CUP) SERVINGS

**QUART-SIZE JAR
INGREDIENTS***

1 cup Great
Northern
white beans

1/3 cup imitation
bacon bits

1/3 cup dried
minced onion

2 tablespoons
chicken bouillon
granules

1 teaspoon
black pepper

1 teaspoon
ground sage

1/2 teaspoon
celery flakes

1/2 teaspoon
parsley flakes

2 cups instant
potato flakes

**ADDITIONAL
INGREDIENTS**

8 cups water

14-ounce can
diced tomatoes

* For pint jar, use half of
the ingredient amounts.

1. To presoak the beans, place them in a microwave-safe container with enough water to cover by 2 inches. Cover loosely with plastic wrap, and microwave for 15 minutes on high power. Or you can bring the beans to boil in a small pot on the stove, and continue to boil for 2 minutes. Turn off the heat and let soak for an hour.

2. Drain and rinse the soaked beans, and place them in a large pot along with 8 cups fresh water and all of the remaining jar ingredients except the potato flakes. Stir well, and bring to a boil over medium-high heat. Reduce the heat to low, cover, and simmer for 1 hour while stirring occasionally.

3. Add the tomatoes, and continue to cook another 45 minutes, or until the beans are tender. Stir in the potato flakes and remove from the heat. Cover and let stand for 5 minutes before serving.

4. Refrigerate any leftover soup in an airtight container for up to 1 week.

CREATINGTHEJAR

Premixed
seasoning packet:

⅓ cup imitation bacon bits

⅓ cup dried minced onion

2 tablespoons chicken bouillon granules

1 teaspoon black pepper

1 teaspoon ground sage

½ teaspoon celery flakes

½ teaspoon parsley flakes

2 cups instant potato flakes

1 cup Great Northern
white beans

For pint jar, use half the ingredient amounts.

1. Wash and thoroughly dry a 1-quart wide-mouth canning jar.

2. Place all of the seasonings in the jar shown at left in a plastic sandwich bag. Place the potato flakes in another plastic sandwich bag.

3. Add the beans to the jar. Using a flat-bottomed object, such as a tart tamper or the bottom of a narrow glass, make the layer as level as possible. Place the bag of potato flakes on the layer of beans, and top with the seasoning packet.

4. Secure the lid, and decorate as desired (see page 24). Attach the instructions for making the soup found below.

Quart-Jar Yield:
12 (1 cup) servings

In addition to the contents of the jar, you will need to add the following ingredients:

8 cups water

14-ounce can diced tomatoes

For pint jar, use half of
the ingredient amounts.

HEARTY POTATO-BEAN SOUP

Place the beans in microwave-safe container with enough water to cover by 2 inches, and cook on high power for 15 minutes. Or bring the beans to boil in a small pot, boil for 2 minutes, and let soak for 1 hour. Drain and rinse the soaked beans, and place in a large pot with 8 cups fresh water and the contents of the seasoning pack. Bring to a boil over medium-high heat. Reduce the heat to low, cover, and simmer 1 hour, stirring occasionally. Add the tomatoes and simmer another 45 minutes, or until the beans are tender. Stir in the potato flakes, remove from heat, and let stand 5 minutes before serving. Refrigerate leftovers in an airtight container for up to 1 week.

MULTI-BEANSOUP

This thick, hearty soup is out-of-this-world delicious! Although the beans require presoaking and the soup must cook for hours, the results are well worth it.

YIELD:
8 (1 CUP) SERVINGS

QUART-SIZE JAR INGREDIENTS*

$1/2$ cup kidney beans

$1/2$ cup black beans

$1/2$ cup red beans

I cup green split peas

$1/2$ cup lentils

$1/4$ cup brown sugar

2 teaspoons chicken bouillon granules

2 teaspoons dried minced onion

1 $1/2$ teaspoons salt

I teaspoon dried parsley

$1/2$ teaspoon black pepper

$1/2$ teaspoon garlic powder

$1/2$ teaspoon celery seeds

ADDITIONAL INGREDIENTS

6 cups water

2 cans (14 ounces each) stewed tomatoes

* For pint jar, use half of the ingredient amounts.

1. Place the kidney, black, and red beans in a medium-sized pot. Add 6 cups boiling water, cover, and soak 8 hours or overnight.

2. Drain and rinse the soaked beans, and place them in a large pot with 6 cups fresh water. Bring to a boil over medium-high heat. Reduce the heat to low, cover, and simmer for $1 1/2$ hours.

3. Add the tomatoes and all of the remaining jar ingredients to the pot. Simmer another 25 minutes, stirring occasionally. Uncover and continue to simmer another 45 to 60 minutes, or until the beans are tender and the soup thickens. Serve hot.

4. Refrigerate any leftover soup in an airtight container for up to 1 week.

CREATING THE JAR

Premixed seasoning packet:
1/4 cup brown sugar
2 teaspoons chicken bouillon granules
2 teaspoons dried minced onion
1 1/2 teaspoons salt
1 teaspoon dried parsley
1/2 teaspoon black pepper
1/2 teaspoon garlic powder
1/2 teaspoon celery seeds

1/2 cup kidney beans
1/2 cup black beans
1/2 cup red beans
1 cup green split peas + 1/2 cup lentils

For pint jar, use half the ingredient amounts.

1. Wash and thoroughly dry a 1-quart wide-mouth canning jar.

2. Place all of the seasonings in the jar shown at left in a plastic sandwich bag. In another sandwich bag, place the split peas and lentils, and shake to mix.

3. Layer the ingredients in the jar as shown at left, pressing firmly with a flat-bottomed object, such as a tart tamper or the bottom of a narrow glass, after each addition. Make the layers as level as possible.

4. Secure the lid, and decorate as desired (see page 24). Attach the instructions for making the soup found below.

Quart-Jar Yield: 8 (1 cup) servings

In addition to the contents of the jar, you will need to add the following ingredients:

6 cups water

2 cans (14 ounces each) stewed tomatoes

For pint jar, use half of the ingredient amounts.

MULTI-BEAN SOUP

Place the kidney, black, and red beans in a medium-sized pot or bowl. Add 6 cups boiling water, cover, and soak 8 hours or overnight. Drain and rinse the soaked beans, and place in a large pot with 6 cups fresh water. Bring to a boil over medium-high heat. Reduce the heat to low, cover, and simmer for 1 1/2 hours. Add the tomatoes, and all of the remaining jar ingredients. Simmer another 25 minutes, stirring occasionally. Uncover and continue to simmer another 45 to 60 minutes, or until the beans are tender and the soup thickens. Serve hot. Refrigerate any leftovers in an airtight container for up to 1 week.

POTATO SOUP

YIELD:
8 (1 CUP) SERVINGS

**QUART-SIZE JAR
INGREDIENTS***

2 cups instant
mashed potatoes

2 cups instant
dry milk

2 tablespoons
chicken bouillon
granules

2 teaspoons dried
minced onion

1 1/2 teaspoons
seasoning salt

1 teaspoon
dried parsley

1/4 teaspoon ground
white pepper

1/4 teaspoon
dried thyme

1/8 teaspoon turmeric

**ADDITIONAL
INGREDIENT**

8 cups water

* For pint jar, use half of
the ingredient amounts.

*This creamy potato soup is ready in just minutes.
I serve it in mugs!*

1. Place all of the jar ingredients in a medium-sized pot. Add the water and stir well.

2. Bring to a boil over medium-high heat, stirring constantly. Reduce the heat to low, and simmer for 3 minutes, or until the soup is thick and creamy. Serve hot.

3. Refrigerate any leftover soup in an airtight container for up to 1 week.

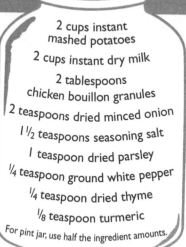

2 cups instant mashed potatoes

2 cups instant dry milk

2 tablespoons chicken bouillon granules

2 teaspoons dried minced onion

1 1/2 teaspoons seasoning salt

1 teaspoon dried parsley

1/4 teaspoon ground white pepper

1/4 teaspoon dried thyme

1/8 teaspoon turmeric

For pint jar, use half the ingredient amounts.

CREATING THE JAR

1. Wash and thoroughly dry a 1-quart wide-mouth canning jar.

2. Layer the ingredients in the jar as shown at left, pressing firmly with a flat-bottomed object, such as a tart tamper or the bottom of a narrow glass, after each addition. Make the layers as level as possible.

3. Secure the lid, and decorate as desired (see page 24). Attach the instructions for making the soup found below.

Quart-Jar Yield: 8 (1 cup) servings

In addition to the contents of the jar, you will need to add the following ingredient:

8 cups water

For pint jar, use half of the ingredient amount.

POTATO SOUP MIX

Place the contents of the jar in a medium-sized pot, add the water, and stir well. Bring to a boil over medium-high heat, stirring constantly. Reduce the heat to low and simmer for 3 minutes, or until the soup is thick and creamy. Serve hot. Refrigerate any leftovers in an airtight container for up to 1 week.

VERYVEGGIE TORTELLINI**SOUP**

Rich in color and flavor,
this soup is satisfying and delicious.

YIELD: 4
(1 CUP) SERVINGS

**PINT-SIZE JAR
INGREDIENTS***

²/₃ cup dried tortellini

¹/₄ cup chopped
sun-dried tomatoes

¹/₃ cup green
split peas

¹/₂ cup dried
chopped carrots

1 tablespoon chicken
bouillon granules

1 tablespoon dried
minced onion

1 ¹/₂ teaspoons
dried basil

1 ¹/₂ teaspoons
dried thyme

¹/₂ teaspoon
garlic powder

¹/₂ teaspoon
black pepper

**ADDITIONAL
INGREDIENT**

5 cups water

* For quart jar, double
the ingredient amounts.

1. Place all of the jar ingredients except the tortellini in a medium-sized pot. Add the water and stir well.

2. Bring to a boil over medium-high heat. Reduce the heat to low, cover, and simmer for 35 minutes while stirring occasionally.

3. Add the tortellini to the pot. Cover and simmer another 10 to 15 minutes, or until the tortellini is cooked. Serve hot.

4. Refrigerate any leftover soup in an airtight container for up to 1 week.

CREATING THE JAR

I tablespoon chicken bouillon granules

½ teaspoon garlic powder

¼ teaspoon black pepper

1 ½ teaspoons dried thyme

1 ½ teaspoons dried basil

I tablespoon dried minced onion

½ cup dried chopped carrots

⅓ cup green split peas

¼ cup chopped sun-dried tomatoes

⅔ cup dried tortellini

For quart jar, double ingredient amounts.

1. Wash and thoroughly dry a 1-pint wide-mouth canning jar.

2. Place the dried tortellini in a plastic sandwich bag.

3. Layer the ingredients in the jar as shown at left, pressing firmly with a flat-bottomed object, such as a tart tamper or the bottom of a narrow glass, after each addition. Make the layers as level as possible.

4. Secure the lid, and decorate as desired (see page 24). Attach the instructions for making the soup found below.

Pint-Jar Yield:
4 (1 cup) servings

In addition to the contents of the jar, you will need to add the following ingredient:

5 cups water

For quart jar, double the ingredient amount.

VERY VEGGIE TORTELLINI SOUP

Place all of the jar ingredients except the tortellini in medium-sized pot. Add the water and stir well. Bring to a boil over medium-high heat. Reduce the heat to low, cover, and simmer for 30 minutes while stirring occasionally. Add the tortellini, cover, and simmer another 15 to 20 minutes, or until the tortellini is cooked. Serve hot. Refrigerate any leftovers in an airtight container for up to 1 week.

Beverages

BAVARIANMINTCOFFEE

PREMIXING REQUIRED

⅔ cup powdered
nondairy creamer

⅔ cup sugar

⅔ cup instant coffee granules

¼ cup cocoa powder

4 hard peppermint candies,
finely crushed

YIELD: ABOUT **48** SERVINGS

For quart jar, double the ingredient amounts.

CREATING THE JAR

1. Wash and thoroughly dry a 1-pint wide-mouth canning jar.

2. In a medium-sized bowl, combine all of the ingredients listed in the jar shown at left. *Premixing is required for this recipe.* Transfer the mixture to the canning jar.

3. Secure the lid, and decorate as desired (see page 24). Attach the instructions for making the coffee found below.

Pint-Jar Yield:
About 48 servings

BAVARIAN MINT COFFEE

*Rich and chocolaty with an invigorating taste of mint,
this very special coffee is the perfect pick-me-up!*

Place 2 level teaspoons of the jar mix in a cup or mug.
Add 6 ounces boiling water, stir well, and enjoy.

CAFÉMOCHA

CREATING THE JAR

PREMIXING REQUIRED

1/4 cup powdered
nondairy creamer

6 tablespoons powdered sugar

1 1/2 cups instant coffee granules

1/4 cup cocoa powder

YIELD: ABOUT **16** SERVINGS

For quart jar, double
the ingredient amounts.

1. Wash and thoroughly dry a 1-pint wide-mouth canning jar.

2. In a medium-sized bowl, combine all of the ingredients listed in the jar shown at right. *Premixing is required for this recipe.* Transfer the mixture to the canning jar.

3. Secure the lid, and decorate as desired (see page 24). Attach the instructions for making the coffee found below.

Pint-Jar Yield:
About 16 servings

CAFÉ MOCHA

*Indulge yourself with this creamy
chocolate-flavored coffee!*

Place 2 level tablespoons of the jar mix in a cup or mug.
Add 6 ounces boiling water, stir well, and enjoy.

ORANGE AND SPICE COFFEE

PREMIXING REQUIRED

1/2 cup + 3 tablespoons powdered nondairy creamer

1/2 cup instant coffee granules

1/2 cup cocoa powder

1/3 cup powdered sugar

2 teaspoons dried orange peel

1 teaspoon cinnamon

YIELD: ABOUT 32 SERVINGS

For quart jar, double the ingredient amounts.

CREATING THE JAR

1. Wash and thoroughly dry a 1-pint wide-mouth canning jar.

2. In a medium-sized bowl, combine all of the ingredients listed in the jar shown at left. *Premixing is required for this recipe.* Transfer the mixture to the canning jar.

3. Secure the lid, and decorate as desired (see page 24). Attach the instructions for making the coffee found below.

Pint-Jar Yield:
About 32 servings

ORANGE AND SPICE COFFEE

This refreshing citrus-flavored coffee has just a hint of cinnamon.

Place 2 heaping teaspoons of the jar mix in a cup or mug. Add 6 ounces boiling water, stir well, and enjoy.

TOFFEE COFFEE

CREATING THE JAR

1. Wash and thoroughly dry a 1-quart wide-mouth canning jar.

2. In a large bowl, combine all of the ingredients listed in the jar shown at right. *Premixing is required for this recipe.* Transfer the mixture to the canning jar, but do not tamp it down.

3. Secure the lid, and decorate as desired (see page 24). Attach the instructions for making the coffee found below.

PREMIXING REQUIRED

1 ¼ cups brown sugar

1 ¼ cups powdered nondairy creamer

¾ cup instant coffee granules

YIELD: ABOUT **64** SERVINGS

For pint jar, use half of the ingredient amounts.

Quart-Jar Yield: About 64 servings

TOFFEE COFFEE

This coffee smells as rich and wonderful as it tastes.

Place 2 heaping teaspoons of the jar mix in a cup or mug. Add 6 ounces boiling water, stir well, and enjoy.

VIENNESE COFFEE

PREMIXING REQUIRED

⅔ cup sugar

⅔ cup instant coffee granules

¾ cup powdered nondairy creamer

½ teaspoon cinnamon

⅛ teaspoon ground allspice

⅛ teaspoon ground cloves

⅛ teaspoon ground nutmeg

YIELD: ABOUT **16** SERVINGS

For quart jar, double ingredient amounts.

CREATING THE JAR

1. Wash and thoroughly dry a 1-pint wide-mouth canning jar.

2. In a medium-sized bowl, combine all of the ingredients listed in the jar shown at left. *Premixing is required for this recipe.* Transfer the mixture to the canning jar.

3. Secure the lid, and decorate as desired (see page 24). Attach the instructions for making the coffee found below.

Pint-Jar Yield: About 16 servings

VIENNESE COFFEE

If you like spiced coffees, this fragrant blend is sure to satisfy.

Place 4 heaping teaspoons of the jar mix in a cup or mug. Add 8 ounces boiling water, stir well, and enjoy.

HOTSPICEDTEA

CREATING THE JAR

1. Wash and thoroughly dry a 1-quart wide-mouth canning jar.

2. In a large bowl, combine all of the ingredients listed in the jar shown at right. *Premixing is required for this recipe.* Transfer the mixture to the canning jar.

3. Secure the lid, and decorate as desired (see page 24). Attach the instructions for making the tea found below.

PREMIXING REQUIRED

2 cups orange-flavored drink mix

1 cup powdered lemonade mix

1/2 cup unsweetened instant tea

1/2 cup sugar

1 teaspoon ground cloves

1 teaspoon ground cinnamon

YIELD: ABOUT **64** SERVINGS

For pint jar, use half of
the ingredient amounts.

Quart-Jar Yield:
About 64 servings

HOT SPICED TEA

Flavored with a blend of orange, lemon, and fragrant spices, this hot tea is the perfect choice on a cold winter day.

Place 2 heaping teaspoons of the jar mix in a cup or mug. Add 8 ounces boiling water, stir well, and enjoy.

SOUTHERNPEACHTEA

CREATING THE JAR

PREMIXING REQUIRED

2 cups sugar

2 cups instant unsweetened tea

6-ounce package

peach-flavored gelatin

YIELD: ABOUT 42 SERVINGS

For pint jar, use half of
the ingredient amounts.

1. Wash and thoroughly dry a 1-quart wide-mouth canning jar.

2. In a large bowl, combine all of the ingredients listed in the jar shown at left. *Premixing is required for this recipe.* Transfer the mixture to the canning jar.

3. Secure the lid, and decorate as desired (see page 24). Attach the instructions for making the tea found below.

Quart-Jar Yield:
About 42 servings

SOUTHERN PEACH TEA

*Serve this drink over a chilled glass of crushed ice
for a refreshing summertime treat.*

Place 3 heaping teaspoons of the jar mix in a tall glass.
Add 8 ounces cold water and stir well.
Add ice and enjoy.

CAFÉVANILLASMOOTHIES

CREATING THE JAR

PREMIXING REQUIRED

1 ½ cups nonfat dry milk

¼ cup sugar

2 tablespoons buttermilk powder

4 teaspoons vanilla-flavored instant coffee granules

4 teaspoons malted milk powder

4 teaspoons instant vanilla pudding mix

4 packages sugar substitute

YIELD: 4 SMOOTHIES

For quart jar, double ingredient amounts.

1. Wash and thoroughly dry a 1-pint wide-mouth canning jar.

2. In a medium-sized bowl, combine all of the ingredients listed in the jar shown at right. *Premixing is required for this recipe.* Transfer the mixture to the canning jar.

3. Secure the lid, and decorate as desired (see page 24). Attach the instructions for making the smoothies found below.

Pint-Jar Yield: 4 smoothies

CAFÉ VANILLA SMOOTHIES

Rich and refreshing, these smoothies have just a hint of coffee and malt.

Place ½ cup of the jar mix in a blender along with 1 cup water and 1 cup ice. Blend until the ice is fully crushed. Pour into a tall glass and serve immediately.

MEXICAN
HOT**CHOCOLATE**

PREMIXING REQUIRED

1 ¾ cups nonfat dry milk

¼ cup cocoa powder

3 tablespoons light brown sugar

½ cup instant chocolate
milk powder

½ teaspoon ground cinnamon

YIELD: ABOUT 20 SERVINGS

For quart jar, double
the ingredient amounts.

CREATING THE JAR

1. Wash and thoroughly dry a 1-pint wide-mouth canning jar.

2. In a medium-sized bowl, combine all of the ingredients listed in the jar shown at left. *Premixing is required for this recipe.* Transfer the mixture to the canning jar.

3. Secure the lid, and decorate as desired (see page 24). Attach the instructions for making the hot chocolate found below.

Pint-Jar Yield:
About 20 servings

MEXICAN HOT CHOCOLATE

*This Mexican-style cinnamon-flavored
hot chocolate is a real treat!*

Place 3 heaping teaspoons of the jar mix in a cup or mug. Add 6 ounces boiling water, stir well, and enjoy.

Metric Conversion Tables

Common Liquid Conversions

Measurement	=	Milliliters
1/4 teaspoon	=	1.25 milliliters
1/2 teaspoon	=	2.50 milliliters
3/4 teaspoon	=	3.75 milliliters
1 teaspoon	=	5.00 milliliters
1 1/4 teaspoons	=	6.25 milliliters
1 1/2 teaspoons	=	7.50 milliliters
1 3/4 teaspoons	=	8.75 milliliters
2 teaspoons	=	10.0 milliliters
1 tablespoon	=	15.0 milliliters
2 tablespoons	=	30.0 milliliters

Measurement	=	Liters
1/4 cup	=	0.06 liters
1/2 cup	=	0.12 liters
3/4 cup	=	0.18 liters
1 cup	=	0.24 liters
1 1/4 cups	=	0.30 liters
1 1/2 cups	=	0.36 liters
2 cups	=	0.48 liters
2 1/2 cups	=	0.60 liters
3 cups	=	0.72 liters
3 1/2 cups	=	0.84 liters
4 cups	=	0.96 liters
4 1/2 cups	=	1.08 liters
5 cups	=	1.20 liters
5 1/2 cups	=	1.32 liters

Conversion Formulas

LIQUID		
When You Know	Multiply By	To Determine
teaspoons	5.0	milliliters
tablespoons	15.0	milliliters
fluid ounces	30.0	milliliters
cups	0.24	liters
pints	0.47	liters
quarts	0.95	liters

WEIGHT		
When You Know	Multiply By	To Determine
ounces	28.0	grams
pounds	0.45	kilograms

Converting Fahrenheit to Celsius

Fahrenheit	=	Celsius
200–205	=	95
220–225	=	105
245–250	=	120
275	=	135
300–305	=	150
325–330	=	165
345–350	=	175
370–375	=	190
400–405	=	205
425–430	=	220
445–450	=	230
470–475	=	245
500	=	260

Index

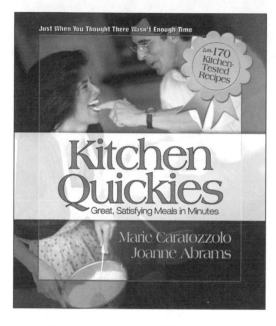

KITCHEN QUICKIES
Great, Satisfying Meals in Minutes
Marie Caratozzolo and Joanne Abrams

Have you ever left work after a long, hard day feeling totally exhausted, but knowing that the second you arrive home, you have to make a meal, *fast*? Or maybe you've spent the day driving your kids from soccer practice to play dates. Now everyone's clamoring for dinner. But is it possible to get a home-cooked meal on the table before, say, midnight? Absolutely!

The authors of *Kitchen Quickies* know that in this busy world, you just don't have time for hours of grocery shopping followed by hours of food preparation. Their solution? To begin with, virtually all of their over 170 kitchen-tested recipes call for a maximum of five ingredients other than kitchen staples. This makes shopping easier. Then the dish itself takes at most forty-five minutes to prepare. And these delicious dishes are actually good for you—low in fat and high in nutrients!

Kitchen Quickies begins by guiding you through the basics of quick-and-easy cooking. Following this are ten spectacular chapters filled with exciting and imaginative dishes, including sensational soups, satisfying sandwiches, refreshing salads, fabulous pastas, tempting chicken and turkey dishes, sizzling seafood, hearty beef and pork fare, meatless delights, enticing vegetable and grain side dishes, and luscious desserts. In *Kitchen Quickies,* you'll learn how to make tangy Margarita Chicken, Savory Crab Cakes, saucy Penne from Heaven, and more—all in no time flat!

So the next time you think that there's simply no time to cook a good meal, pick up *Kitchen Quickies.* Who knows? You may even have time for a few quickies of your own.

$14.95 • 240 pages • 7.5 x 9-inch quality paperback • 2-Color • 16 Full-Color pages • ISBN 0-7570-0085-1

THE SOPHISTICATED OLIVE

*The Complete Guide to
Olive Cuisine*

Marie Nadine Antol

Simple. Elegant. Refined. With a history as old as the Bible, the humble olive has matured into a culinary treasure. Enter any fine restaurant and there you will find the sumptuous flavor of olives in cocktails, appetizers, salads, entrées, and so much more. Now, food writer Marie Nadine Antol has created an informative guide to this glorious fruit's many healthful benefits, surprising uses, and spectacular tastes.

Part One of *The Sophisticated Olive* begins by exploring the rich and fascinating history and lore of the olive—from its Greek and Roman legends to its many biblical citations to its place in the New World. It then looks at the olive plant and its range of remarkable properties, covering its uses as a beauty enhancer and a health provider. The book goes on to describe the many varieties of olives that are found around the world, examining their oils, flavors, and interesting characteristics. Part One concludes by providing you with everything you need to know to grow your own olive tree—just like Thomas Jefferson.

Part Two offers over one hundred kitchen-tested recipes designed to put a smile on the face of any olive lover. It first explains the many ways olives can be cured at home. It then covers a host of salads, dressings, tapenades and spreads, soups, side dishes, entrées, breads, cakes, and, of course, beverages to wind down with. So whether you are an olive aficionado or just a casual olive eater, we know you'll be pleased to discover the many new faces of *The Sophisticated Olive.*

$13.95 • 204 pages • 7.5 x 7.5-inch quality paperback • 2-Color • ISBN 0-7570-0024-X

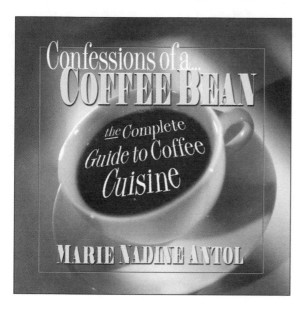

Confessions of a Coffee Bean

The Complete Guide to Coffee Cuisine

Marie Nadine Antol

Yes, I have a few things to confess. But before I start, I just want you to know that I couldn't help it. It just happened. Everywhere I went, they wanted me. Now, I have a few things to share—I think it's time to spill the beans.

With a distinct aroma and an irresistible flavor, it has commanded the attention of the world. It is the coffee bean, and while many seek its pleasures, few know the secrets of its origin and its appeal, and the key to getting the best out of the bean. Designed for lovers of coffee everywhere, here is a complete guide to understanding and enjoying this celebrated object of our affection.

Part One of Confessions of a Coffee Bean opens with the history of coffee and details the coffee bean's epic journey from crop to cup. It then describes the intriguing evolution of the coffeehouse, highlights surprising facts about coffee and your health, and provides an introduction to the most enticing coffees available today. Finally, this section presents everything you need to know about making a great cup of coffee, from selecting the beans to brewing a perfect pot.

Part Two is a tempting collection of recipes for both coffee drinks and coffee accompaniments. First, you'll learn to make a wide variety of coffee beverages, from steaming brews like Café au Lait to icy concoctions like the Espresso Shake. Then, you'll enjoy a bevy of desserts and other coffee companions, from classic crumb-topped cakes to coffee-kissed creations such as Rich Coffee Tiramisu. You'll even find recipes for coffee-laced candies and sauces.

Whether you're a true coffee aficionado or just someone who loves a good cup of java, this is a book that will entrance you with fascinating facts about all things coffee.

$13.95 • 204 pages • 7.5 x 7.5-inch quality paperback • 2-Color • 0-7570-0020-7

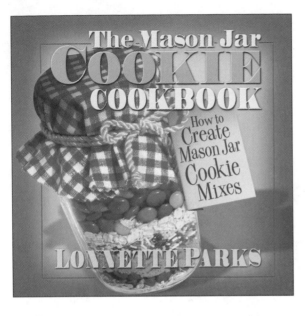

THE MASON JAR COOKIE COOKBOOK

How to Create Mason Jar Cookie Mixes

Lonnette Parks

Nothing gladdens the heart like the aroma of cookies baking in the oven. But busy lifestyles have made it increasingly difficult to find the time to bake at home—until now. Lonnette Parks, cookie baker extraordinaire, has not only developed fifty kitchen-tested recipes for delicious cookies, but has found a way for you to give the gift of home baking to everyone on your gift list.

For each mouth-watering cookie, the author provides the full recipe so that you can bake a variety of delights at home. In addition, she provides complete instructions for beautifully arranging the nonperishable ingredients in a Mason jar so that you can give the jar—complete with baking instructions—to a friend. By adding just a few common ingredients, such as butter and eggs, your friend can then prepare fabulous home-baked cookies in a matter of minutes. Recipes include Best Ever Chocolate Chip Cookies, Blondies, Cranberry Dream Drops, Gingerbread Cookies, Oatmeal Raisin Cookies, and much, much more.

Whether you want to bake scrumptious cookies in your own kitchen, you'd like to give distinctive Mason jar cookie mixes to cookie-loving friends and family, or you're searching for a unique fund-raising idea, *The Mason Jar Cookie Cookbook* is the perfect book. It just may bring home-baked cookies back in style.

$12.95 • 144 pages • 7.5 x 7.5-inch paperback • 2-Color • ISBN 0-7570-0046-0